"Tim Askew's *Th[...]* [...] powerful, origina[...] [...] real opportunity a[...] [...] pathway of being an Entrepreneur. Askew has a delightful combination of erudition, eloquence, vulnerability and joy."

Tracy Goss, NY Times best-selling author of *The Last Word on Power*

"I love, love, love *The Poetry of Small Business* and recommend it if you already find joy and meaning in your work-or if you are looking to do so. Tim's book will make your heart sing!"

Carol Kinsey Goman, Forbes columnist and the author of *The Silent Language of Leaders: How Body Language Can Help - Or Hurt - How You Lead*

"Tim Askew writes about entrepreneurship with startling honesty, insight and perspective. Read and revel in his experience."

Ken Tencer, CEO, Spyder Works Inc. and bestselling co-author of *Cause a Disturbance*

"Tim Askew communicates with a compelling and eloquent soulfulness rare in business writing."

Neil Smith, NY Times best-selling author of *How Excellent Companies Avoid Dumb Things*

"Askew outlines powerful steps to take organizations and individuals to great success and meaningfulness. This book is clearly written from the heart and with clear conviction. A great read for any accomplished or aspiring entrepreneur or manager."

Kevin Sheridan, NY Times best-selling author of *Building a Magnetic Culture*

"Timothy Askew is an entrepreneurial artist who is one part Plato, one part William F. Buckley and one part Billy Graham. He is profound, thought-provoking and insightful."

> Michael Drapkin, CEO, XB5 Risk Management, author of *Three Clicks Away; Advice From The Trenches of Ecommerce*

"Tim Askew is the 'Accidental Entrepreneur' who became a 'Conscious Capitalist.' Askew provides a wise, practical, honest perspective to how one can build a successful sales career while nourishing one's soul."

> Michael Strong, co-founder Conscious Capitalism, lead author *Be the Solution: How Conscious Capitalists Can Solve All the World's Problems*

"This book is wonderful! Elegant, honest, inspiring. Not your usual business and management tome."

> Melissa Maxey Wade, Professor and Executive Director, The Barkley Forum, Emory University

"Tim is the right type of entrepreneur. Someone who believes and has experienced the fact that you can do well and do good at the same time. *The Poetry of Small Business* is a gripping tale of business as personal salvation and a great lesson for all business leaders."

> Paul Spiegelman, Founder, Inc. Small Giants Community and Chief Cultural Office, Stericycle

Tim Askew has found the voice of the voiceless entrepreneur, sometimes afraid of the rising sun, sometimes emboldened with great powers, but human above all else. That's what you'll discover in The Poetry of Small Business.

> Lewis Schiff, Author of *The Middle Class Millionaire*

The Poetry of Small Business

An Accidental Entrepreneur's Search for Meaning

By Timothy Askew

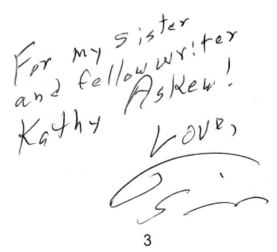

For my sister
and fellow writer
Kathy Askew!

Love,

For my dear daughter, Truitte Rose Askew.

Table of Contents

Foreword

Searching for Salvation

> *"There are all kinds of addicts, I guess.*
> *We all have pain. And we all look for*
> *ways to make that pain go away."*

- Sherman Alexie

Becoming an entrepreneur has done a lot more than pay the bills over the years, it's saved my life. It took me a while to admit this, but I spent many years as a committed addict of several sorts. Without detailing the specifics of this, suffice it to say I was at times a liar, a thief, a drunk, a seducer, a narcissist, a scofflaw, and a devotee of magical thinking. I was a wastrel using my innate gifts, education, and background to avoid reality and personal growth, hide my authentic core, and avoid an engaged life. I was a creature of ashen hollowness living in the shadows of a moral and mental abyss, a soulless Gollum caught in a vertiginous descent into life-killing compulsion and escapism.

I was not unaware of my fallen state, but felt quite like St. Augustine, who famously prayed, "Lord, take this sin (read lust, compulsion, addiction) from my heart—but not yet." I told myself I could give up my addictions at any time, as long as it was next Tuesday. Nevertheless, at a nadir I had to stop or spiritually die. I chose to come to a dead stop with the help of the usual suspects—twelve-step programs, friends, family, faith, and therapy. But most importantly to me, I discovered, quite by accident, a new vehicle of salvation in which to pour a repairing soul. For me, that vehicle was entrepreneurship.

The formation of my executive sales outsourcing firm, Corporate Rain International, was an attempt to simply create a company that would allow me to live healthily inside it. Yes, I needed to make a profit, but my primary purpose was to become useful and whole and sustainable in rebuilding a personal center. For me, that meant staying honest with myself and others.

My addictions were close kin to my series of failures in life. I started out to be a minister or teacher or professor. Something ennobling and service oriented. I actually was on the road to a Ph.D. in philosophy, but I dropped out to become an actor for 10 years, where, despite appearances in a couple of Broadway shows and a national soap opera, I basically crashed and burned, supporting myself mostly on unemployment and bartending. (Being an actor was also like catnip to my addictive nature. It was like putting Miracle-Gro on my character defects.) I tried to sing opera for two years and totally failed. I tried to produce a Broadway show and lost a ton of money.

As I approached 40, I was broke and didn't know what the hell I wanted to do. Quite out of the blue, a CEO, who I knew socially, asked me to represent him around some high dollar discreet business matters. It was essentially a customized, high-level sales job. The very idea of sales made my gorge rise. What was sales? Used car sales? Glengarry Glen Ross? A corporate Willy Loman? I had no business training, no sales training, and no interest in being a corporate cog. But the offer was from a friend, so I tried it.

Lo and behold, I was a tremendous high-level salesman. And I loved it. I saw a niche in executive sales outsourcing and formed a company around the idea. It worked. Out of the maelstrom of confusion, chaos, and bleakness in my life to that point, I became a successful entrepreneur. Entrepreneurship offered me a unique lifesaver and a shot at personal redemption. It gave me a magical palimpsest reset to my life of addiction and failure. It allowed me to banish demons and pour myself into a profit-making service vocation, fraught with meaning and value. And money. It was the ultimate

10

therapy, offering the where-with-all for a life awash in grace and earned dignity. A life after death, so to speak. Thus, for anyone struggling with vices or finding their purpose in life, entrepreneurship can be a Godsend. It is a gift quite separate from its value as a vehicle of capitalist striving. If I went bankrupt tomorrow, I would be a success as an entrepreneur because I have grown courageous, passionate, free, and whole through living in my company and serving its corporate community and clients. For me, owning my own business has been about meaning, integrity, recovery, and usefulness, during times when I needed it more than ever. My gratitude for the institution of entrepreneurship is beyond words.

As a recovering addict and as a multiple failure, my daily business life offers me a spiritual home and a locus for centered growth and earned satisfaction. This is the goal and chief reward for my personal business journey. One of the many insights of AA includes the suggestion of shifting out of your addiction through substitution. My small business is The Good Addiction.

So addiction and failure can be the handmaidens of success, when mediated through the leavening antidote of entrepreneurship. While the bad stuff doesn't go away, it is transmogrified into new and useful experience through

11

productive enterprise. I am convinced we are all addicts and failures to a lesser or greater degree. Why not let your business be your salvation?

Introduction

Most folks I know think the purpose of business is to make money and amass wealth. It can be that. A healthy business makes money. But that is not what the purpose of my life as an entrepreneur is about, and not what this book is about. This book is about business as a vehicle for meaning. It's about the business journey as a reward in itself.

I have experienced the entrepreneurial process as a deeply personal gift, an accidental and unexpected grace, and a fecund loam for soulfulness, growth, and healing. While earned lucre has paid the mortgage and more, for me, profit is not the raison d'etre for my fulfilling business life. I am a successful entrepreneur to the extent my life has become whole, free, honest, and healthy.

While I want to share whatever insights may exist from my nineteen years of small business experience as CEO of my accidental company, Corporate Rain International, this book is intended as an intuitive, anecdotal record of thought and experience. It is an attempt to offer a personal, alternatively valid, non-traditional business philosophy of entrepreneurship.

This book evolved from the weekly blog I started several

years ago called, "Making Rain: The Idle Thoughts of an Accidental Entrepreneur." What these years of weekly thought pieces turned out to be was a series of observations on a picaresque and autodidactic business journey. These essays more and more became a record of a businessman not primarily interested in business, per se. While business has been a good living, the entrepreneurial process, more importantly, has been a cornucopia of constantly deepening self-knowledge, ethical growth, humor, and love. It is a vital, primary relationship in my life, existing in parallel to my personal life.

This book is about vocation. It is about business as a vehicle of calling, centering, and service; of finding integrity, worldly meaning, personal dignity, and spiritual reality through an activity most would identify as quotidian and earthbound. But for me, business is not that. I have found a passion, a home, and a psychological freedom in business that is usually associated with the arts and religious faith.

Indeed, my personal antecedents are mostly in the performing arts and in religion. I never studied business or economics in college or graduate school. In fact, until the last few years, I had never read a book on business, per se. My entry into the business world was much like Alice tumbling down the rabbit hole. To my surprise, like Alice, I had entered a world of wonderment where all my assumptions were turned upside down. I've been in that world for nearly 20 years now. My business life is a happy accident.

This book is my take on business. It is not about profit, spreadsheets, money, management, or financial success. It's a book about how I have experienced business as grace. My hope is to inspire other entrepreneurs to experience more grace in their businesses as well.

Part 1: The Entrepreneur

Modern Frontiersmen

America has historically been a frontier society. "Go west, young man," Horace Greeley famously intoned. But what do you do if your country has the imagination of a frontier nation but has no physical frontier left to conquer? There is only one obvious outlet that comes quickly to my mind: Entrepreneurship. That is today's new frontier. It is a wondrously good fit for the courageous risk-taker who no longer has the unexplored American West, or the mysterious deepest, darkest Africa, or the longing to reach the moon.

There are several reasons the mythos of the entrepreneur has so captured the popular imagination. It is certainly the allure of the cultural frontier ethos (self-made man hews out a place for himself in the raw wilderness.) But I believe it's about more than that. Entrepreneurship is a most elusive concept. It's scary and exciting and foreign to most people. It takes a unique type of person to pursue it as a career and lifestyle choice and actually be successful.

I believe almost all entrepreneurs are hard-wired for passion, individualism, and an unshakable thirst for freedom. For those who stumble into entrepreneurship without those qualities, they may gain them as their business evolves. (For most, it's painful, if not impossible to go back to working for someone else after you've worked for yourself. Entrepreneurship becomes part of a fully lived life.)

Part of the passion that drives people to own their own business comes from a deeper level of consciousness. It is a rather visceral longing to create meaning itself. We live in an anomic world that has little of the cohesive, society-knitting homogeneity of the past. Our's is a restless, unmoored society that has no real outlet for the Ayn Randian business hero, the existential voyager. It is a world comfortable with irony, but bereft of spiritual essence—a world where the best and brightest increasingly compete for positions as bureaucrats and oligarchs.

In such a world, entrepreneurship can engage the soul of those who long to find a human center, and I would argue, even a theological center, to anchor their reason for being. For example, there is almost an apotheosis that has occurred around Steve Jobs, Elon Musk, and other entrepreneurial heroes—a sort of low-level semi-deification of the innovative business striver.

We're in a brave new world that longs for Truth, even if we are inarticulate and unclear in that longing. Entrepreneurship is the real-life modern gamification of the hero's search for the Holy Grail. A new business is a self-created church for some. It is a grotto of escape from the meaninglessness of the quotidian, a defiance of the amorphous new normal. Society has come to a place very similar to where William Butler Yeats was when he spoke into the political and economic vacuum between World Wars I and II:

"Things fall apart, the center cannot hold,

Mere anarchy is loosed upon the world,

The blood-dimmed tide is loosed, and everywhere

The ceremony of innocence is drowned;

The best lack all conviction, while the worst

Are full of passionate intensity."[i]

Entrepreneurs hope they can at least create a personal fulcrum where the center *can* hold. They hope to create their own sea of tranquility, clarity, and personal satisfaction—inured to societal dysfunction.

The Poetry of Small Business

Types of Entrepreneurs

"Everything in this world is created by neurotics. They alone have founded our religions and composed our masterpieces."

- Marcel Proust

Most successful entrepreneurs I know fall into two categories:

1. The disruptive, ambitious, aggressively growing entrepreneur.
2. The lifestyle entrepreneur.

The first is the widely recognized and admired heroic entrepreneur who takes risks to create disruption and big financial payoffs. The second is the more sedate, though still successful businessman. The lifestyle entrepreneur is interested in creating and sustaining enough innovation and differentiation to ensure a comfortably dependable cash flow and ROI, but who is less interested in visionary, precarious business adventure.

But I would submit there is a third, less common type of successful entrepreneur. This is the entrepreneur who lives for the coin of "mattering" as well as earning a living, for being whole and worthy of the privilege of having lived freely and meaningfully. This third type of entrepreneur is becoming even more important, because frankly, I believe entrepreneurship is becoming less financially lucrative. The fertile seedbed of freedom, ideal for thriving creative business, is being eroded by an encroaching hegemony of the triumphalist oligarchic state—a state well-intended but innately inefficient and hostile to the economically disruptive, independent, and seminal. Carl Schramm, formerly of the Kaufman Foundation, reports a troubling economic trend: a decline in the formation of new businesses. Schramm notes that approximately 700,000 firms came into existence each year in the 2000s, but only 500,000 so far this decade.[ii] Steve Wynn and Bernie Marcus unequivocally aver they could never have created, respectively, Wynn Resorts or Home Depot if they had to begin in today's increasingly suffocating, bureaucratic control economy.

Luckily, these conditions don't discourage the third type of entrepreneur. This third class of entrepreneur measures their success not on the soulless tundra of pure wealth seeking, but on a business' ability to create community, meaning, dignity, independence, and happiness, as well as fortune. This reward is a richness of being, not merely a worth of wealth.

The hidden secret value of entrepreneurship is *vocational*, in the religiously foundational sense of the word. Meaning an entrepreneur's life can be lived effectively and significantly, as part of the great oneness of all existence and truth, which is often called God. Since we're discussing types of entrepreneurs, I'm just going to throw it out there that I think all entrepreneurs are a little crazy. I know I am. And you know what? I'm pretty sure it helps to be a little crazy if you want to build and run a business.

Here's a secret: I am not the world's best businessman. I'm just not. Part of the inadequacy of my basic business background is chosen; I simply don't enjoy administration, spreadsheets, human resources, or quantitative analysis. What does interest me are the more elusive values of entrepreneurship—the envisioning, the individuality, the strategy, the philosophy, the ethics, the creation of culture, and the collegiality of it. What I want out of my business is no less than freedom, truth, and salvation. I want entrance into that metaphorical Golden City On The Hill, what Shakespeare calls "the brightest heaven of invention."[iii] I think great entrepreneurs (and I am most assuredly not one) have this procrustean longing and intent. In this myopically secular age, many business founders are perhaps inchoately and unconsciously involved in a closeted, low-level search for God.

Certainly that was the case with Steve Jobs. Walter Isaacson wrote about it in his biography of Jobs.[iv] Jobs was more than a bit nuts. And I mean that in the nicest possible way. Maureen Dowd, in a *New York Times* op-ed, referred to Jobs as a "monstre sacré." She says, "his life sounded like the darkest hell of volatility."[v] A bipolar madness. Jobs was truly a great entrepreneur. But he was also partly a mad neurotic, an activist, and an avid spiritual searcher and seeker of ultimate truth. Because he sought to find his spiritual center in his business, it doesn't mean he was a nice man. He was difficult, bullying, and arrogant. His spiritual entrepreneurial journey did not make him Mother Theresa. Yet like Moses, Jesus, and Captain Kirk, he went boldly where no man had gone before. Ultimately his business journey was a uniquely autodidactic search for personal meaning and God in a non-religious age.

Maybe a deep search for meaning in life is, in itself, madness. But it's often the only way to create something truly unique and to find fulfillment.

Here is what Plato said about poetry, but it could apply equally to the heart of the true entrepreneur:

"...If any man come to the gates of poetry without the madness of the Muses, persuaded that skill alone will make him a good poet, then shall he and his works of sanity with him be brought to naught by the poetry of madness..."[vi]

Education

> *"There are these two young fish swimming along and they happen to meet an older fish swimming the other way, who nods at them and says, 'Morning, boys. How's the water?' The two young fish swim on for a bit, and then eventually one of them looks over at the other and goes, 'What the hell is water?'"*
>
> **- David Foster Wallace**[vii]

Although the entrepreneurial spirit and drive for deeper meaning are something that can't be taught, by nature, the role often falls within the realm of business pedogogy—something that is often rooted in formal education. Skills like statistics, accounting, and management are part of entrepreneurship, but they are all tiny parts of a much larger picture. Mastering these parts can be useful, but it in no way guarantees the other parts will be within grasp. I find it remarkable that there is a proliferating and profitable business in teaching hundreds of thousands of "insta-presto" parvenu entrepreneurs in business schools. It's a bunch of snake oil hooey to my mind. (There are nearly 2,000 full-time professors of entrepreneurship today who are putting out putative entrepreneurs, while every year new company formation steadily declines.[viii]) It is a case of academia's taking advantage of the deep longing for autonomy and personal meaning among students, who don't realize that entrepreneurship is not an academic skillset, but a spiritual frontier for the intrepid.

Clearly I am partial to learning from experience. However, I find it interesting that well-respected people and media outlets are starting to follow my reasoning. One reason for this is because of the specialization engrained in higher education. If you want to be an entrepreneur, steer away from specialization. It is the enemy of the new and disruptive and the true. This has never been more relevant than it is now. All aspects of enterprise are changing like lightning. And this will do nothing but speed up.

"A human being should be able to change a diaper, plan an invasion, butcher a hog, command a ship, design a building, write a sonnet, balance accounts, build a wall, set a bone, comfort the dying, take orders, give orders, cooperate, act alone, solve equations, analyze a new problem, pitch manure, program a computer, cook a tasty meal, fight efficiently, die gallantly. Specialization is for insects."

- Robert Heinlein

Ur-entrepreneur Steve Jobs, in his speech introducing the iPad in 2010, said the following: "It's in Apple's DNA that technology alone is not enough. It's technology married with liberal arts, married with the humanities, that yields the results that make our hearts sing."[ix]

In a like vein, *The Wall Street Journal* recently had an article on the increasing dangers of training for specific vocational skill sets and niches in higher education. The current common wisdom is that general education (the liberal arts) is quaintly old-fashioned and impractical. As such, college has become narrowly defined as specific job preparation, not as something designed to educate the whole person. A glorified vocational training. Hence the increasing dominance of STEM (Science, Technology, Engineering, Math) education. The WSJ limns the counterintuitive argument that this is exactly the wrong approach for long-term hireability.[x] And that, I think, applies in spades to prepping an incipient entrepreneur.

Today's jobs, problems, and needs are almost certain to change radically and rapidly. A hot job in today's marketplace, say in mobile marketing or hospital finance or pharma management, may (and probably will) become dead meat with the next technological permutations, regulatory changes, or innovative disruptions. The best training for all of us is in how to think globally and objectively about the future, about what's around the bend. And that means being a broadly trained thinker and citizen of the world, as well as a specialist in specific verticals of product or service. A generalist sees the forest as well as the trees and knows how to adapt nimbly and flexibly with a view to the big picture and main chance. That's pretty crucial for an entrepreneur.

Harking back to the previously cited WSJ article, Anthony Carnevale of Georgetown University's Center on Education and the Workforce calculates that the current unemployment rate among recent IT graduates at the moment is actually twice as high as that of theater majors.[xi] Not what you expect, huh? There has been a paradoxical phenomenon going on in the job market for several years now. With the economic downturn, we've had huge unemployment and underemployment rates (between 14% and 18% by various estimates), yet hundreds of thousands of jobs go begging. These unfilled jobs require high-levels of technical and scientific skills that have unfortunately been lacking in the work force. This created an almost panicked stampede by university students, facing unemployment, to put on blinders and focus strictly on jobs available in our brave new world of austerity and job paucity. The problem is that people aren't stopping to realize that a massive influx of professionals who have the same niche skills isn't going to help the job market much either. Furthermore, in teaching only the "how," students will miss out on the bigger picture "why"; the legacy of centuries of human wisdom from whence emanates truly fresh, world-changing business creativity and human truth. There is a danger here, especially for the future of entrepreneurship.

Since my own background is in the arts and I never trained for business, I am perhaps prejudiced toward what I see as resourcefulness and resiliency imbued by a broad generalist experience and education. But I do believe that successful business innovation is much more aligned with creative calling than any specific skillset. Creative business must be a combination of learned craft and intuitive art.

Michael S. Malone, a Forbes columnist and author of the book The Guardian of All Things: The Epic Story of Human Memory, wrote an op-ed in the Wall Street Journal titled "How to Avoid a Bonfire of the Humanities."[xii] It speaks to this conundrum. Malone recounts one of his university colleagues, who teaches

English, saying, "There are parents who tell their kids they will only pay tuition for a business, engineering, or science degree." I can only imagine this phenomenon increasing as parents cope with their unemployed progeny moving home. (And also coping with a growing threat of student loan defaults, often leaving retired parents holding the bag. Many shocked and unfortunate parents have even lost their homes as a result of co-signing on defaulted student loans.[xiii] No wonder they are trying to steer their children in what they believe to be the most lucrative direction.)

Although higher education and the economy aren't perfectly lining up, there may be some practical hope for the humanities emanating from Silicon Valley, of all places. Malone recounts somewhat timidly asking his successful entrepreneurial friend Santosh Jayaram if he would mind putting in a few good words for the humanities to members of his professional writing class at Stanford, who were considering changing majors.

Santosh said, "Are you kidding? English majors are exactly the people I'm looking for." He explained: "Twenty years ago, if you wanted to start a company, you spent a month or so figuring out the product you wanted to build, then devoted the next 10 or 12 months to developing the prototype, tooling up and getting into full production... These days this work can be contracted out to programmers anywhere in the world, who could do it in a couple of weeks. But to get to that point, he said, you must spend a year searching for that one undeveloped niche that you can capture. And you must use that time [to build your company] without having an actual product...And how do you do that?" Santosh said. "You tell stories. The battleground in business has shifted from engineering, which everybody can do, to storytelling, for which many fewer people have real talent."

"Maybe stories are just data with a soul."
- Brene Brown

But what is the practical lesson for the currently practicing entrepreneur in Malone's article? Well, for me, the key lesson is the increasing importance of storytelling—the ability to bring creativity, poetry, passion, and metaphor together to recruit employees, strategic partners, investors, and, of course, customers to join your company. Maybe that is my ultimate job as a founder and CEO of my firm—to be the Storyteller-In-Chief.

I frequently listen to Garrison Keillor's *Prairie Home Companion* on the weekends. He is eternally joking about the un-employability of English majors. While there is no doubt that college English departments are in decline, perhaps there is still a future for the liberal arts major as a business leader who can call on the non-quantitative intuitions of history, music, art, philosophy, and faith with a creative flexibility, rather than just technical expertise. The new entrepreneur will be a person who can tell and retell evolving business stories, synthesizing and communicating new concepts and creations, and adjust quickly and empathetically to a changing international world.

Perseverance

"Home, I'll go home… After all
tomorrow is another day."

- Scarlett O'Hara in *Gone With the Wind*

For me, one of the joys of fatherhood is discovering the insights and simple wisdom of children's literature. I used to love reading to my daughter Truitte Rose when she was young. She had a favorite book titled *Alexander and the Terrible, Horrible, No Good, Very Bad Day* by Judith Viorst. My daughter couldn't get enough of this book, which chronicles a day in the life of a boy where nothing goes right.

So, what does this have to do with entrepreneurship? Well, I too had a very bad day once at my own firm, Corporate Rain International. I sat down at my chair and was assaulted by the following:

1. Fighting a cold.

2. Dealing with a client crisis.

3. Resolving a minor credit card fraud.

4. Losing a valued employee.

5. My ex-wife's complaint about a late alimony check.

6. Having to read a dense legal contract.

On the side of my desk was a veritable Mt. Everest of unanswered sales calls. And all this before noon. I was having a terrible, horrible, no good, very bad day. I've learned that days like this can be quite dangerous—not because of the circumstantially difficult day, but because of my reaction to it. On such a day I feel I have to push hard to compensate—to move, move, move—to rush, rush, rush. And when I give in to this feeling, I make poor judgments. I make mistakes. I insult people and lose my temper. My whole mien becomes frenetic, faked, forced, and charmless.

As an owner, it's hard to slow down when Rome is burning all around you. (Only you can prevent this forest fire!) I've had to learn the efficacy of hitting the pause button—of not trying to be more than I am. And, especially, I've had to learn *not* to make crucial decisions on such days.

When I have a very bad day, everything emanates from a dark, bleak, shrunken part of my soul, where I exist only as a miasma of utter insufficiency: That place where dwells the cowed and frightened child, and the cornered rat. So my "professional" response is to assume the trappings of a sanguine, competent businessman and fumfer through. But, in fact, the real good me is not present. The fact is that on a terrible, horrible, no good, very bad day I am in reality one dark, primordial, primal scream—a lost Edvard Munch template and an enraged troll.

Over the years I've lost money, sales, friends, and reputation on days like this, while grinding my teeth and determinedly…getting…it…all…done. I have frequently caused myself harm under the guise of dutifully and manfully doing my duty to capitalist enterprise. Only slowly have I overcome such hubristic folly.

One of the best and kindest pieces of advice I ever received was from an elderly Portuguese friend named Leonardo. (He was a fellow waiter where I was working at the time.) After observing me in a moment of intense frustration and self-flagellation, Leonardo took me aside, sat me down, put his hands on my very tense shoulders, and said simply, "You can not push the river, Timothy. Flow with it." That's all he said.

I think it's hard for any entrepreneur to follow that advice.

We *live* to push the river. But the simple fact is we really can't force our will on any number of things.

So what's the answer to the terrible, horrible, no good, very bad day? Well, I guess my answer to that conundrum is increasingly to just stop, no matter how much I have to do. As Scarlett O'Hara says at the end of a very bad day in *Gone with the Wind,* "Home, I'll go home...After all, tomorrow is another day."

When I was in college I remember being depressed and distraught over a failed love affair. My mother was appropriately sympathetic, of course. That's a mother's job. But then she told me, "You know there's little I or anyone can say that will cheer you up, Timothy. There's only one thing I know to do on really dark days. The only thing I know to do is spend that day just cleaning my toilets."

Productivity

"There is time enough for everything in the course of the day, if you do but one thing at once, but there is not time enough in the year, if you will do two things at a time. "

- Lord Chesterfield

Dr. Edward Hallowell, a specialist in ADD/ADHD treatment, wrote a book in 2007 called *Crazy Busy*. In it he identified something called the "attention deficit trait" (ADT), which he posited was rampant in today's business world, which has the same symptoms as ADD. He says, "Never in history has the human brain been asked to track so many data points."[xiv] Our busyness has only increased exponentially since Hallowell wrote those words.

I think the entrepreneur has an especial vulnerability to this ADT. I'm a fairly hyper person, which isn't an uncommon state for an entrepreneur. Additionally, unlike most normal jobs, entrepreneurship is never nine to five. There are an infinite number of things we could all usefully do every day. (The day I am not up to my ass in alligators is the exception.) So it is easy for business owners to embrace an omnipresent multitasking mode made possible by constantly advancing technology.

Though it may be counter intuitive to the credo of most entrepreneurs, I've personally found a multitasking frenzy ain't the answer to this conundrum. To understand why, we should look to the origin of the word "multitasking." It was originally applied to describe the parallel processing capacities of computers. The term was transferred to the human attempt to do as many things as possible, as fast as possible, as if the computer model was applicable to human abilities. Personally, this flittery, fast-paced "skill" often leaves me with the breathless sense that I am missing the bigger picture: of seeing the trees but not the forest. Perhaps I'm just a dullard, but what occurs when I rush to get everything done in the seemingly inadequate time frames I'm presented with is that I pay a price. And this is particularly true in the micro niche of my specialty, executive selling, where I find refinement, service, and attention to detail especially important. The personal price I pay for speed always shows in my work, whether through accuracy, quality, verboseness, or oversimplification—there is always a diminution in one of these areas. That loss of precision is particularly a negative in presenting a compelling sales tonality to a corporate leader. Casual mistakes can sink you with those folks. When I'm in a rush, the answer is to slow down.

For me, multitasking is really an information overload that withers my success and efficiency.

Apparently, I am not alone. There is growing scientific evidence that people who excessively multitask retain much less than those who take in information in a more sedate and focused manner. Consider the work of Dr. Patricia Greenfield, a professor of developmental psychology at UCLA. She warns in a *Science* article that our growing use of the Internet, with all its advantages of speed and accessibility, "seems to be weakening our "higher order cognitive processes [including] abstract vocabulary, mindfulness, reflection, inductive problem solving, critical thinking and imagination.["][xv]

No wonder my brain feels slower on social media—it *is* slower. Growing evidence continues to show that multitasking is really a shallow flitting over the surface of numerous subjects or ideas. Former Microsoft VP Linda Stone describes this as "continuous partial attention" and notes this is "a common affliction of executives," constantly scanning for opportunities and staying on top of contacts, events, and activities in the effort to miss nothing.[xvi] And the research of Dr. Russell Poldrack of the University of Texas has frequently proselytized that multitasking adversely impacts how you learn. He says, "We have to be aware that there is a cost to the way that our society is changing, that humans are not built to work this way. We're really built to focus. And when we sort of force ourselves to multi-task we're driving ourselves to perhaps be less efficient in the long run even, though it sometimes feels like we're being more efficient."[xvii]

What multitasking actually does is allow us to engage in fast but shallow thinking. Flitting from social media flower to flower is disassembling our ability to think deeply about the meaning of life in general, as well as dampening the deeper creativity needed for an evolving, innovative business. Our information and knowledge base may be growing, but what we add in trivial facts surely weakens us all in integrated wisdom. (Hence our need for the restoratives of meditation, quiet, reverie, and even idleness—to palliate our ability to deeply focus, and to regularly escape from the spiritually vitiating gulag of a multitasking ADD Nation.)

One of my concerns about multitasking in our burgeoning online world (especially social media) is simply the time it sucks up, and how it distracts. How many online miracles and digital wonderments can I absorb? I personally find an overabundance of data makes important things fuzzy and harder to find. It actually impedes good decision-making and my business intuition. That's why my attentiveness to Facebook, Twitter, and LinkedIn is intentionally not up to speed with many other professionals. But you know what? My business is sailing smoothly. Making sure social media is not a priority creates time for me to think about the stuff that matters: empathy, understanding, and subtlety in all my sales outreach. I have time to work on important projects, RFPs, or let business communication marinate before I respond. As an entrepreneur, this is an important part of success.

Here is one of the best pieces of advice you'll ever get: Don't speed read social media news streams whenever you have a "free" moment, or let them distract you throughout the day. Concentration is king, and the speed gained through multitasking is the enemy of doing core entrepreneurial chores well.

Part 2: The Business

Culture

"The least of things with a meaning is worth more in life than the greatest of things without it."

- Carl Jung

Building a business is hard. Not only in terms of developing something customers want to buy, but organizing your company in a way that makes people want to work there. With seemingly endless options in the world, why should employees choose to support *your* business day after day?

Here's a name for you: Mihaly Csikszentmihalyi. Try pronouncing that one! (It's a Hungarian moniker. Sounds like cheek-sent-me-high-ee.) Dr. Csikszentmihalyi is professor of Psychology at Claremont Graduate University in California, where he heads the Quality of Life Research Center. He doesn't write directly about entrepreneurship or sales, per se, but he does speak to the issue of meaning in business eloquently and scientifically. And there are certainly corollary implications for sales in his work, which centers on the study of happiness, personal efficaciousness, and creativity. To wildly oversimplify Dr. Csikszentmihalyi's work, he writes about what creates value, meaning, and happiness in business and work. Among other things, he tackles the question of what makes a business life worth living, and what makes life itself worth living. While all of this has heavy academic undertones, the relevancy to entrepreneurs is quite simple: you need to give your employees a reason to work for you.

I have just scratched the surface of his work, and I won't insult Dr. Csikszentmihalyi with my limited understanding, but he writes well, accessibly, and with the humility and humor of a true seeker. For example, to give just a hint of his tonality and concerns, in his book *Good Business,* he quotes Norman Augustine, the former CEO of Lockheed Martin: "I've always wanted to be successful. My definition of being successful is contributing something to the world…and being happy while doing it…You have to enjoy what you're doing. You won't be very good if you don't. And secondly, you have to feel you are contributing something worthwhile…If either of these ingredients are absent, there's probably some lack of meaning in your work."[xviii] One of my recurring tropes and passionate beliefs is that there is a great underestimation of the importance of meaning in employees' lives. Any company will win in the long-term by projecting an institutional concern where employees' well being is equally as important as profit. After all, how would you make money without any workers? To show how much I truly believe in this, I will confide in you a guiding principle I use to run my business: Communism.

Communism certainly isn't usually the first word that people use when they talk about building business culture. At least not in the U.S. I, however, look to communist ideals for upholding a happy, nimble company. Though a failed governing system in historical practice, I attempt to mould Corporate Rain International as close as possible on a communist archetype. (Or at least as close as one can get to that and still be a committed, passionate Ayn Randian capitalist.)

This is not the *prima facie* paradox it seems. My firm, of course, as all companies, must make money to survive and prosper. But it operates with a dual goal of creating meaning in tandem with making money—the former being the genesis of the latter.

44

This is becoming a somewhat less radical notion. Harvard Business Review recently reported a longitudinal study conducted by Sigal Barsade and Olivia (Mandy) O'Neill titled, "What's Love Got To Do With It?" Barsade and O'Neill describe the business efficacy of what they call a culture of "companionate love." In a nutshell, their research shows employees reported much higher levels of commitment, satisfaction, teamwork, and personal and corporate health in a culture of warmth, safety, and personal growth.[xix] (Well duh, as my daughter would say.)

> *"If you wish to achieve worthwhile things in your personal and career life, you must become a worthwhile person in your own self-development."*
> **-Brian Tracy**

While this type of culture may be easiest to institute in a small company, it is increasingly being achieved in larger, well-known organizations, as well. Note that PepsiCo lists "caring" as the first guiding principle on its website.[xx] Tony Hsieh's Zappos states as a core value, "We are more than a team…we are family, watch out for each other, care for each other and go above and beyond for each other."[xxi] And maybe it's a lucky accident, but meaning and culture surely drive happiness in my sales associates, my employees, and myself.

In a world frequently populated by rogues and thieves masquerading as benign capitalists, and in a world increasingly dominated by coldly efficient technology— oriented toward dehumanizing, distancing, and quantifying those pesky customers—branding one's company as humane and caring in all the simplest human interactions is invaluable.

So, here are my six personal principles for creating what I call a "communist capitalist" model for corporate health:

1. **Good is greed.** Michael Douglas, as "Gordon Gekko" in *Wall Street*, famously said, "Greed is good." He had it exactly backwards—*Good is greed*. For the long-term entrepreneur, goodness and service make the putative rewards of business greed—money, success, status, and happiness— much more likely. Customers sense and smell goodness. They want to be around it and touch it—and most importantly, buy it. They intuitively trust it more than all the quantification analysis and sales exposition in the world. Goodness builds reputation, good will, and value for the long term. It isn't Pollyannaish to want to do good in the world; it's believing in what goes around

comes around. Karma is practical greed. Being genuinely open and unselfish from the depth of your being is ultimately the selfish way to be, if you consider long-term repercussions. This is a through-branded corporate belief in my company.

2. **A company of equals.** I mean this quite literally. I don't think I'm smarter or more talented than the people I hire. This includes administrative professionals and employees in other task-based roles. I hire people who I can learn from. I strive to create a flat management culture of decentralization, where each member is her own CEO. We have a culture of "micro bosses" that are under a constantly reinforced rubric of assumed common ethics and a radical orientation of customer care.

3. **The purpose of the organization is personal growth for all members and clients.** Following the idea of "companionate love" in the aforementioned study, employees need to be in a job where they can grow. When they reach a plateau where they are no longer learning, the job is no longer a good fit for them or for the organization. I believe in this so strongly that I

lovingly encourage my valued executives to move on when they begin to outgrow my firm. Over the past 19 years, I've had four sales executives leave to become corporate VPs of Business Development at other firms, as well as two executives leave to become successful entrepreneurs. I'm very proud of that. All are still friends.

4. **Love.** Many people are uncomfortable talking about love in the workplace, but it does have its place. Tim Sanders wrote a wonderful book several years ago called *Love is the Killer App*, which was seminal to developing my perspective on creating my own company culture. Corporate commitment to love as an overarching principle effortlessly evinces itself as a specific trope of consistent customer care and service throughout a corporation.

5. **Giving back.** Specific corporate acts of eleemosynary generosity make a company stronger. In my firm's case, we give away a free three-month business development campaign to a small, deserving non-profit each year.

6. **Lived CEO leadership, example, and guidance.**
My personal struggle with addiction 19 years ago
led me to form my company based
in strengthening my own principles of recovery.
Specifically, I wanted to create a community that
would bring me happiness and satisfaction, and
enjoy the spiritual journey with a group of kick-
ass fellow travelers. I believe bone-deep good
leadership is grounded in the permeation of
personal values, shown in the small and consistent
everyday acts of each owner and entrepreneur.

**A Case Study on Goodness: Danny Meyer,
Restaurateur and Founder of Shake Shack**

*"The wise man does not lay up his own treasures. The
more he gives to others the more he has for his own."*

- Lao-Tzu

I have always believed that money is as much a bi-
product of goodness as it is of technical business
prowess. Restaurateur Danny Meyer is a good man. He is
a living testament to my frequently voiced mantra, "Good
is Greed." Or, as Danny puts it, "Generosity is clearly in
our self-interest."

What a sweet guy. (And a wily, tough, successful

businessman.) He is a relaxed, almost impish fellow, full of bonhomie, unfeigned humility, and self-directed humor. He is both playful and unpretentious.

Meyer is the CEO of Union Square Hospitality Group in New York. He owns some of the most respected eateries in the United States. They include Union Square Cafe, Gramercy Tavern, Blue Smoke, and Jazz Standard, as well as the rapidly expanding upscale burger chain, Shake Shack, with multiple locations nationally.

I personally have zero interest in cooking or creating food (though I love to eat and am a member of the James Beard Foundation), but could palpably feel Meyer's passion for both food and business philosophy. He wrote quite a fine book called *Setting the Table*, which should be read by any business owner interested in creating culture. The book is a compelling memoir of a master restaurateur, as well as a thoughtful and moral creator of business culture. While Danny's book covers the ins and outs of food, the pedagogical value for the entrepreneur is his thinking about branding through what he defines as "hospitality."

He states, "Service is the technical delivery of a product. Hospitality is how the delivery of that product makes you feel." Meyer says the key to creating a hospitality culture is your employees. They are more important to Meyer than his clients. He says if you take care of your employees, they will take care of your customers. He starts by hiring people with the emotional skills of empathy and genuinely liking people. His hierarchy of importance is employees, customers, community, suppliers, and investors—in that order.[xxii] I couldn't agree more.

In addition to his missionary zeal for hospitality, I believe the key insight for entrepreneurs is his deep commitment to giving back. He is a person of a karmic faith that the universe gives back to you what you put into it. His greatest entrepreneurial success to date is Shake Shack. He attributes this success to nothing more than his five year pro bono commitment to clean up the rat infested, run-down Madison Square Park in New York City. He is overly modest and the story is too long for this chapter, but suffice it to say, Danny Meyer is a man who walks his talk.

Meyer calls his foundational philosophy "hospitality," but I call it simple goodness and decency. Or, at the risk of sounding treacly, *love*—truly the selfish way to practice successful enterprise.

Here's a bit of advice I like from *Setting the Table*.
"Wherever your center lies, know it, name it, stick to it,
and believe in it. Everyone who works with you will
know what matters to you and will respect and appreciate
your unwavering values."[xxiii]

Hiring Philosophy

"Inventors and men of genius have almost always been regarded as fools at the beginning (and very often at the end) of their careers."

- Fyodor Dostoevsky, **The Idiot** *(1869)*

My philosophy about employees is this: I don't want employees at all. What I want are peers with a congruent value system to share my journey. For me, that journey must begin with common values. I seek out sales associates who want their work to give back to the world through service and truth-telling. Under that rubric of shared values, I try to only hire colleagues who genuinely care about the client, and genuinely care about getting efficacious results.

The truth is, we all have different ways of showing this caring and getting things done. So I organize Corporate Rain International as a lifestyle firm, a virtual company that affords all associates the freedom to maximize their own sales instincts and acumen with minimal interference from the big bad boss (me). Over the years, I've found this philosophy makes for an enlivened company and a happy community. It incentivizes and vivifies autonomy as a core value.

Etymologically, the term "autonomy" derives from the Greek word meaning self-governing. To be autonomous means to act in accord with oneself. When we are autonomous, we all emanate a salesmanship infused with energy, integrity, and, most importantly, a personal authenticity that sells. Authenticity is compelling. Like the anecdotal story about the judge who, when asked to define pornography, said, "I can't define it, but I know it when I see it." Buyers feel much the same way. They know authenticity when they see it. I see incentivizing authenticity in every sales associate of my firm as a primary leadership imperative. You want to activate authenticity not just because it is moral, but because it is effective.

Authenticity results from employees who share your corporate values; they uphold your values not because they are told to do so, but because they genuinely believe in them too. In my case, I hire educated, value-oriented salespeople who are self-starters, and I turn 'em loose within a controlled system. And then I trust in the Lord. The results have generally rewarded my faith. Of course, everyone works for money. That has to be fair and appropriate. But I firmly believe that passion and commitment are not fundamentally incentivized by money. They are better motivated by happiness, personal integrity, and autonomy.

Eccentricity

"Do not fear to be eccentric in opinion for every opinion now accepted was once eccentric."

- Bertrand Russell

I love eccentric people. I must admit I am partial to hiring them. And it has almost always paid off for me. When you can harvest a bounty of original personalities, you often have something special indeed. Yes, original people are often arrogant, blunt, erratic, and moody. But they are oh so wonderful. They offer an extraordinary value to the employer who can stomach them. Personally, I can not only stomach them, I truly swim in the joy of their company. I am enlivened by their intuition, their humor, their integrity, and frequently, by their love.

The big problem with hiring creative, independent folks is managing them. I have a whole company of these folks. People often ask me how I can manage them as a boss. Well, the short answer is I basically don't manage them. I coax them, I spoil them, I admire them, and I love them. I let them fail and grow—and mostly succeed. My risk is leavened by the fact that I only hire people who I think are smarter than me. I want a company of CEOs. I only ask them to have a moral core, a commitment to my culture and community, and to follow simple administrative processes. I seldom need to fire my associates.

So how do you engage, utilize, and retain these creative, questing souls? Here are six specific suggestions for harnessing eccentricity:

1. **Give creatives meaningful work.** Creatives often think about the bigger issues in life, the forest as well as the trees. Only give them interesting, challenging projects and clients. Give them the hard stuff.

2. **Trust them.** Assuming they are ethical and diligent, let them fumfer their own way to success. Give them the freedom and flexibility to flourish. Don't force them into undue structure or quotas. It obviates the very reason you hired them.

3. **Be flexible.** If they excel, let them do it their way. If they create superb results working five hours a week in their underwear at home when you are paying them for 30 hours in the office, who cares?

4. **Give them a sense of ownership.** Ask their opinion and take their advice seriously. Make them feel valued, an essential part of the organism that is your company.

5. **Don't expect to motivate them through money.** Of course pay them fairly, but research indicates these out-of-the-norm employees may actually be discouraged and perform poorly when they are rewarded just for completing a task.[xxiv] And note what that irreplaceable wise man of motivation and happiness, Mihaly Csikszentmihalyi, says in his classic book, *Flow*: "The most important quality, the one that is most consistently present in all creative individuals, is the ability to enjoy the process of creation for its own sake."[xxv] Indeed.

6. **As a caveat, do not promote employees who are pure creatives to managers.** Necessary responsibilities change at the manager level. Pure creatives aren't always interested in these tasks or inclined to be good at them.

"If a sufficient number of management layers are superimposed in top of each other, it can be assured that

disaster is not left to chance"

- Norman Augustine

After considering this instruction manual for managing what I consider to be the best type of employees, you might be wondering if it's really worth it. Wouldn't it be easier to hire regular corporate-types who live by following complex processes and rules? The ones who live for daily status updates and communicate primarily via PowerPoint?

If you want to sacrifice innovation, progress, agility, and a healthy appetite for risk at your organization, sure, go ahead. Hire corporate-types. See if I care. Just a fair warning: My experience with that type of employee is that they are primarily about protecting their asses. They are not about the new. They are not about the cutting edge. They are about keeping their jobs. Unless you want people who can only follow orders rather than think for themselves, avoid these job candidates like the plague. When Jeff Bezos hired a search firm to staff his aborning and disruptive company, Amazon, he was reportedly asked what he was looking for in an employee. Supposedly, he responded, "Give me your wackos." Amen, Brother Jeff. Me too.

Incentivizing Staff

"[In speaking about motivation] the proper question is not, 'How can people motivate others?' but rather, 'How can people create the conditions within which others will motivate themselves."

- Dr. Edward Deci, Why We Do What We Do

Good business owners help motivate all employees, but salespeople are a particularly important segment of the workforce, since profits depend directly on their hard work. Many strategies have been used over the years to incentivize salespeople, but it almost always comes down to lucre, material possessions, and free vacations. Perks. Business leaders must think salespeople are either stupid or shallow. Actually, I do believe much of what is expressed about incentivizing the salesperson emanates from underestimation, condescension, and even contempt for that person and her profession. Good salespeople are not testosterone-driven Darwinian manipulators or sociopaths, as they are so often portrayed. That's why I rarely read sales books. They make me mad. From my own experience as an executive salesman, I believe most sales managers approach the whole subject of sales incentivization ass-backwards.

Many salespeople fail to reach their goals or quit within the first year. While the reasons for this are complex, I believe the overemphasis on monetary reward is a large part of the problem.

Good employees, particularly salesmen, like good entrepreneurs, are creatures of individuality, subtlety, and nuance. They like being part of something that gives their life and their world meaning. They are not molded by the desire to become filthy rich. Good ones are intuitive, freedom-loving cowboys who have a competitive streak. While a good salesman may be able to "sell ice to an Eskimo," that does not mean he is so cynical he wants to do that or that it makes him happy, fulfilled, or incentivized to do that. Salespeople want more from their jobs. That's how I feel personally, and that's why I've shaped my business as an ethical sales and service community. I followed my instincts in doing this because it felt right, and I have begun to discover I am not as odd or alone in my approach as I had always assumed. Even more amazingly, there is an increasing body of scholarly research that supports the instincts I followed in conducting my business in a manner I damn well felt like. (God bless entrepreneurship.)

Business owners should note the recent work of happiness researchers Elizabeth Dunn and Michael Norton, who found that additional income buys us little additional happiness once we reach a comfortable living standard. They quote a Princeton study using Gallup polling data from almost a half million American households that shows money creates little beneficial effect after reaching the $75,000 mark.[xxvi]

This validation is particularly true in the realm of sales incentives. My core assumption has always been that happy people don't fundamentally work just for money; I don't operate that way, so I figure other people don't either. They work for satisfaction, happiness, appreciation, a free life, and other non-quantifiable benefits. This research confirms that higher monetary incentives are not necessarily the carrot that should be dangled before top salesmen to maintain an increased effort. Sales has to be approached on the basis of long-term sustainability and corporate mission, not excessive near-term monetary motivation.

Edward Deci, author and Director of the University of Rochester's Human Motivation Program, agrees with this perspective. He says, "When people say that money motivates, what they really mean is that money controls.

And when it does, people become alienated—they give up some of their authenticity—and they push themselves to do what they think they must do.*"xxvii*

If you really want to motivate your salespeople, try recognizing them publicly. At a recent NYC Capital Roundtable seminar I attended, Pericles Mazarakis, managing director at the venture capital firm Thomas H. Lee Partners, acknowledged a need for more non-monetary thinking around sales incentivization. He told a story of an incident he observed at Remington a number of years ago. A certain sales director at Remington kept his staff's efficiency and enthusiasm high, not by monetary carrots or demanding quotas, but by the simple expedient of placing a Xeroxed sheet on the desks of salesmen who did well, saying, "Great job! You are killing it!" The consulting firm looking at the company found that these cheap Xerox sheets were being framed by these salesmen and meant more than any quantitative reward. Employees felt good their efforts were noticed by a manager, and they were proud of their achievements. This demonstrates how people want to be part of an organization that imbues their lives with quality and meaning, and gives them a sense of personal accomplishment. Yes, they need to make money, but I don't believe it ever activates their ardor and deep commitment. It does not inspire full use of their internal resources, their full being, or their passion.

The next time you want to motivate your salespeople (a good time is probably now), try saying a heartfelt thank you. Recognize them in front of other coworkers so their colleagues see how well the team is doing. Chances are, they will remember this type of reward more than a few extra dollars in their paycheck.

Choosing the Company You Keep

"Quality attracts quality"

- Oscar Nunez

Never lie down with dogs. You may get fleas. There is a crucial differentiation to be made for any entrepreneur by the company he keeps. It defines a businessman and his firm every bit as much as his business plan and marketing. I say that not as some sort of clinch-jawed, nose-in-the-air snob, but as a practical man of business. From the inception of any enterprise, it is important to conceptualize the long-term defining nature and implications of commercial partnerships and associations. Those companies and people you service and associate with will have implications for your own and your company's reputation.

Both in terms of process and execution, it is a time-saver and efficiency-producer to assume that the basic values of your company and those you serve are the same. It is always an anxious thing to try to fit a square peg into a round hole; it creates a strain. Even if it is a subconscious tension, a simple adumbration of uneasiness, conflicting or incongruent corporate value systems will impinge on the focused energy needed for collegial business success. As an entrepreneur, it is important to know who you are and understand your company's core value. Without this self-awareness, how would you know what constitutes a congruent client? A corporate culture is influenced by the cultures of those whom you choose to serve, as well as by your internal dynamics. In other words, quality attracts quality.

Clients and employee associates are drawn to a tone, an ethos, an aura. For long-term success you need to define, establish, and hold dear a set of core beliefs that permeate your organization. To quote Ray Liotta as Shoeless Joe Jackson in the movie Field of Dreams, "If you build it, they will come." If you build it right and present it effectively, you will create long-term clients among kindred spirits. And you will not attract those you should not align with, which is appropriate and an important business value.

The Secret to Luck

"When a man is a favorite of fortune she never takes him unawares and, however astonishing her favors may be, she finds him ready."

- Napoleon Bonaparte

As I mentioned, I was once an actor and singer. Not a common background for a businessman, so people tend to remember it. Although I had a performing career that was more bartending than Broadway, business friends and clients sometimes send their sons and daughters to me for advice if their progeny want to go into show business.

These kids almost always ask, "What's the most important thing about making it as a performer?" My answer? LUCK. There are a multitude of truly talented young artists, and honestly, I find luck the key differentiator in their success. This answer usually brings a thoughtful frown from young people, who undoubtedly expected me to credit something they feel is within their control, like hard work or education. Sure, those things are great too, but luck is the real factor. It's deeper than that, though. The secret is to be *ready* for luck to happen, if and when it does happen.

The same is utterly true of entrepreneurship. Successful entrepreneurs are driven and courageous. They are a passionate, hard-working breed. I truly love entrepreneurs. They are never boring people. But, despite their admirable, if disparate, natures and work habits, I still believe the key element in their success is luck.

How does luck happen? In my opinion it comes to those who are most comfortable in their own skin. It comes most easily to those who live and breathe their unique selfness. There is an achieved existential integrity to people who have luck. They are themselves. Becoming a real "self" is, of course, a life-long process, but it is just as important as marketing, business plans, spread sheets, technological know-how, and everything else they teach you in B-School. For the entrepreneur, I actually believe becoming one's true self might be more important that anything taught in school.

There is wisdom in the phrase, "It's better to be lucky than smart." Luck defies encapsulation and control. It is an ineffable and recondite goddess. But it seems to me that luck comes to those who are soulfully open to accepting fate's surprises. I believe it happens to people who've somehow developed an innate subconscious integrity that allows them to pivot adroitly and automatically in response to any happenstance.

I was lucky last year. On the train, I bumped into a neighbor, a man I've known passingly for a good while. We got to chatting about neighbor things and quite incidentally, I mentioned that my firm sets up elite sales initiation pipelines for corporate clients. Well! It turns out my neighbor represents a major foreign country, and he is responsible for guiding his nation's many entrepreneurial companies in penetrating the U.S. market. Who'd 'ave thunk it? The next day he had me in front of nine CEOs at his consulate's boardroom. Within five days, three of those companies were clients. God bless Metro North.

In this case, I can thank luck, but also something bigger: being ready to connect with the people around me. I didn't have my earbuds in. I wasn't looking down at my phone while the world blindly passed me by. I wasn't fighting my surroundings and trying to control them or turn them into something else. I was living in the present and ready to experience whatever the world wanted to give me that morning. I was going with the flow.

Maybe being lucky is simply going with the flow and noticing the random opportunities that other people miss.

While I believe this wholeheartedly, the idea of randomness is a hard concept for a lot of people to accept. It's unpredictable, and that makes people uncomfortable. Author Nassim Taleb explores this concept in some of the books he's written, including *The Bed of Procrustes, Antifragile: Things That Gain From Disorder*, and most famously, *The Black Swan: The Impact of the Highly Improbable*. Taleb is what I would describe as an anti-intellectual intellectual. He's a curmudgeonly thinker and sceptic who believes in common sense and learning through experience. Kind of like most entrepreneurs.

He says, "We humans, facing limits of knowledge, and things we do not observe, the unseen and the unknown, resolve the tension by squeezing life and the world into crisp commoditized ideas."[xxviii] He posits that man, in his longing for certainty, artificially invents grand economic theories that simply cannot take into account the randomness and unpredictability of reality. He believes realistic trial and error beats academic knowledge every time.

"We live on the brink of disaster because we do not know how to let life alone. We do not respect the living and fruitful contradictions and paradoxes of which true life is full."

- Thomas Merton

For Taleb, the greatest business sin is to be a "fragilista," a person who weakens the institution he works in because he thinks he knows what's going on. These folks believe they can conquer randomness, that they can control and prevent game-changing "Black Swan" events. They create more and more rigid structures and rules that support their confident sense of control and mastery. Taleb's epiphany is that this is a foolish chimera that actually undermines what they claim to be buttressing. He believes top-down planning guarantees inflexibility, inefficient complication, and delays. It predictably results in the downfall of companies and governments, whenever they turn their destiny over to central planners.

Taleb fundamentally stands the quality of uncertainty on its head, declaring that the unpredictable is both desirable and healthy. The "antifragile" company is an alive, existential company that benefits from the adversities, uncertainties, and stressors that challenge it.

By implication, Taleb is a capitalist Darwinian. He clearly believes in the idea of "creative destruction" advanced by the Austrian economist Joseph Schumpeter, which is that all things are improved when shocked—that wolves are fundamentally good for the elk herd because they winnow out the weakest members, creating a stronger genetic and practical future for the species. Or, in entrepreneurial terms, restaurants are eternally failing, resulting in constantly improving cuisine. If failing restaurants were somehow protected (or bailed out) from the random judgments of the marketplace, the result would be bland food and the end of innovation. The parallel implications of government bailouts on the macro-economic scale are obvious.

I could easily go on about Taleb's message, but enough said. In practical terms I'd sum it up as simply this: shit happens. Beautiful things happen. Go with it.

"The individual never asserts himself more than when he forgets himself."

- Andre Gide

Randomness may seem scary, but it's actually a true blessing. Believing in randomness is the first step in realizing you can't control the universe. You are merely a cog in something much larger. When you stop trying to control the uncontrollable, something beautiful happens. It makes you free. It keeps you in the present. It gives you license to be real. It allows the unexpected to occur. It makes the world funny and a delight. It imbues you with spontaneity and focus.

How do you get started in adapting this mindset? *Give up.* That's right, give up. Every day. It's not a bad thing to do before you begin your sales day. Have no hopes and no testosterone-fueled, hegemonic expectations. Just begin to work. Let your day unfold naturally while doing your best in the moment rather than worrying about what's to come.

In *Forbes* Magazine, sports shrink Bob Rotella uses this advice on athletes. He advises them to "be like Manny Ramirez" when he was with the Boston Red Sox. Before the World Series, Ramirez famously said he didn't care if the Red Sox won or lost; it wouldn't be the end of the world. Ramirez took a lot of heat for his statement, but Rotella says Ramirez' statement is insightful in that it showed his understanding of the need for relaxation.[xxix] Being present in the moment allows for maximal focus in athletic achievement as well as business.

Sales is one of the least predictable and controllable of business functions. Success in sales is a result of many intangibles. It is not like analyzing a spread sheet. Successful sales come from instinctive, almost primitive, attributes among its quality practitioners. Perhaps a combination of charm, real caring for and sensitivity to other people, and a fierce, even vulpine, push for a final closing. These paradoxical qualities must exist simultaneously in a master salesman.

I know there is an army of sales experts out there who disagree with me. Their sales systems are legion and variegated. But, unlike many other vocations, sales does not lend itself to iron control. Nor does entrepreneurship. If you're a control freak, entrepreneurship ain't for you.

It can be overwhelming to sit down to a new business development project. To create something out of nothing. To aggressively start to fill in a tabula rasa. It is an act of faith. Yet if you begin, the work takes its own form. Spontaneity, though, can make sales and business process such fun—a joy, a revelation. Being open to luck and watching things unfold without knowing what's going to happen---to me, that's entertainment. Even in rejection. And rejection will be the major result of most of any salesman's efforts. (At least it is of mine.) Good things do happen if you create space for spontaneity, for freedom, for truth, for humor, for joy. It allows for the non-rational to happen. Going with the flow is its own reward. It allows for miracles in the world of entrepreneurship.

Embracing Failure

"Success is stumbling from failure to failure with no loss of enthusiasm."

- Winston Churchill

One my employees recently came to me and inquired about "the secret sauce" of what made me a successful entrepreneur. I recall my rather pompous and condescending reply had something to do with bromides like hard work, honesty, preparation–the usual suspects. But my employee interrupted me saying, "No, no, no. I want to know that special, personal thing you do that makes you really good." After stuttering a minute, the only thing I could come up with was that I got good by being quite bad–over and over again.

I'm a failure, many times a failure. It's probably the most salient fact about me as an entrepreneur. Whatever success has happened in my business life is directly related to my many failures: failure as an academic, failure as an actor, failure as an opera singer, failure as a Broadway producer. And failure is my friend. I learned this early on in my acting career. One of the key things an actor must be good at (besides acting) is dealing with rejection. An actor must accept rejection on a daily basis. He deals with constant and personal failure through rejection. It's a *splendid* preparation for owning a business. Put simply, to survive my actor's life I had to find satisfaction not in the occasional success—actually getting a role—but in the process of auditioning itself.

> *"Our business in life is not to succeed, but to continue to fail in good spirits."*
> **- Robert Louis Stevenson**

Likewise in owning a business and driving sales, happiness must be found in the process, as well as the results. When you go for the sale and fail, you should enjoy it and have fun. How does one do that? Sometimes going big makes it more exciting. An acting colleague named Austin Pendleton taught me this long ago. I remember Austin talking about solving his auditioning conundrum—the problem of how to figure out what directors really were looking for. He told me what he had finally decided was to "go big" with his audition choices. If he had an "outrageous failure" at least he was rejected for something distinctive.

Over 20 years later, I still think back on that comment

whenever I have to confront failure. There is a thrill in being brave, which makes facing rejection more fun. I was recently reminded of the "go big or go home" approach to failure when I came across an article in the *Wall Street Journal* titled "Better Ideas Through Failure."[xxx] It features a story about Amanda Zolten, a Senior VP at Grey Advertising, doing a courageously creative pitch for a kitty litter product.

Zolten's inspiration for the pitch came from her cat, Lucy Belle. Before Zolten and her team met with six of the company's executives, she buried Lucy Belle's mess in a box of the company's litter and pushed it under the conference-room table. No one noticed until Zolten pointed it out. Shocked, several executives pushed back from the table. Two left the room. After a pause, those who remained started laughing, says Zolten. "We achieved what we hoped, which was creating a memorable experience." she says. She proved her point effectively— no one had smelled it.

Zolten's boss, Tor Myhren, named Ms. Zolten the winner of his first quarterly *Heroic Failure* award for "taking a big, edgy risk."

There is a wonderful lesson for the entrepreneur here. A

compelling, charismatic sales narrative comes out of fearlessness and free expression of the truth. Not to mention the respect that fearlessness garners from others. (Considering this, it's easy to see how being brave creates a feeling of adequacy and fulfillment, even in the face of rejection.)

There's something about persevering through adversity that makes people deeply likable. This journey is where failures turn into role models and heroes.

One of my favorite failures is R.A. Dickey, a former baseball player for my beloved team, the consistently lowly New York Mets. (Now he's a member of the Toronto Blue Jays, as of this writing.) I love R.A. Dickey. He is old for an athlete (over 40!) and deeply formed by multiple failures, sadness, and hard knocks. He is a man who has had an unexpected and accidental life. He is an inspiration and is a shining beacon for what is achievable, even out of the embers of a fallen, inadequate, and heavily scarred life experience.

> *"Ever tried. Ever failed. No matter. Try again. Fail again. Fail better."*
>
> **- Samuel Beckett**

Dickey wrote an autobiography called *Wherever I Wind Up*. All company creators and entrepreneurs should read it. It's well-written and not at all your usual self-congratulatory jock tome. To briefly sum up Dickey's riveting story, he describes his life as one long recovery from depression, childhood sexual abuse, brokenness, and frequent thoughts of suicide. He describes himself as a "picture of mediocrity" until he discovered the vehicle of his salvation, the knuckleball. But even more important is his courage and humility in describing the very personal process of becoming a fully realized and whole man.

After being a high draft choice out of Tennessee, it was discovered that Dickey was missing a key elbow ligament needed to stabilize his pitching arm. He bounced around several major and minor league teams for many years, until out of desperation; he took up the knuckleball, a pitch that only a handful of men have ever learned to handle effectively.[xxxi]

In a lovely essay in the *New York Times*, his old teammate and friend, Doug Glanville, describes the knuckleball as "a joystick-controlled UFO" of a pitch, totally unpredictable in its trajectory to the batter, but also unpredictable to the pitcher himself.[xxxii] It is a joyous goofball-accident of a pitch.

"A good knuckleball has no spin, at least not the one that acts like the butterfly that just drank enough cocktails to be over the legal drinking limit. And it's slow enough, and frozen enough, so you can see the letters on the ball. But it's no comfort reading those letters, since you have absolutely no idea where they're going."[xxxiii]

So, how can Dickey inspire the entrepreneur? He is a triumph of autodidactic bootstrapping, as well as practical humility. Like most of us entrepreneurs, he was bad before he became good. He's been quoted saying he isn't a self-made man, but that is not completely true, as endearingly unpretentious as Dickey may be. He has made a journey into freedom, wholeness, and authenticity that is also the pursuit of most of the effective entrepreneurs I know. Entrepreneurship can be a vehicle for personal salvation, much as Dickey's knuckleball saved his life and career. I personally think of the entrepreneurial company as, much like the knuckleball, an unpredictable butterfly of unexpected twists and turns—but still an infinitely rewarding vehicle of meaning and happiness for those with the courage to ride it.

Dickey is a Christian, but to me he is a true Zen Buddhist master of living in the present. He is a specific inspiration and existential hero to me, as an entrepreneur. So Dickey is one of my favorite failures. We should all be willing to fail so well.

Loneliness

"The most terrible poverty is loneliness."

- Mother Teresa

Lonely. God, that word sounds pathetic. It's not the first thing that comes to mind when pondering the entrepreneur, but it's a reality that exists. It certainly does for me. Most folks think of owners and CEOs as hard driving, autonomous, tough, and energetic. Mini-masters of the universe. And most of my business peers are that, in their different ways. However, I believe there is a closeted yearning in most of us to connect communally, safely, and discretely.

Sometimes personal issues arise from professional success. Friendships, for entrepreneurs, are hard. We're busy. In our limited "free" time, most of us have primary commitments to our families and homes. We can't even keep up current friendships. Most of our human contact is within our own firms. However, it is simply not practicable to have real, open friendships with employees, even top executives. Being a boss requires a certain distance.

One of my all-time favorite TV series is *The Sopranos*. Tony Soprano is kind of an entrepreneur when you think about it. I remember an early episode where Tony is worried about being yessed to death by his gang. He asks his wife Carmela what she thinks. She replies, "[Your subordinates] compliment you on your new shoes. They tell you that you're not going bald. You think they really care? You're the boss, they're scared of you. They have to kiss your ass, laugh at your stupid jokes."[xxxiv]

Unfortunately, Carmela is utterly right.

Unlike non-entrepreneurs who often make friends at work, we don't have that luxury. And making friends outside of work as an adult is hard. It requires time we simply don't usually have. An easeful, peer community of shared assumptions and base experience is increasingly rare in our balkanized society. Yet the soulful amelioration of personal business aloneness is not a need that an owner should repress or shove aside lightly. I have personally gotten a good helping of intimate, discreet camaraderie from my colleagues in NYC who are fellow entrepreneurs at the Inc. Business Owners Council (members of the Inc. 5000), but I have heard of it coming from church business groups, therapy groups, or fraternal volunteer organizations.

Part 3: The Sale

Sliminess

"There are worse things in life than death. Have you spent an evening with an insurance salesman?"

- Woody Allen

I was recently forwarded a blog post from one of my employees about the T.V. show *Mad Men*. The posting was essentially a fan letter to fictional character Don Draper, proclaiming him the best salesman of all time on television. However, the blog concluded with a list of other things he was great at, such as being one of the best "salesmen, con artists, sweet-talkers, swindlers, and bullshitters." Wow.

The juxtaposition and equivalency of salesmen with scammers is breathtaking. And yet it fully reflects the popular view of salesmen as somewhat lower than whale shit. The list of examples from movies includes such luminaries as:

- Gordon Gecko (portrayed by Michael Douglas in *Wall Street*)
- Blake (portrayed by Alec Baldwin in *Glengarry Glen Ross*)
- Freddy Benson & Lawrence Jamieson (portrayed by Steve Martin and Michael Caine, respectively, in *Dirty Rotten Scoundrels*)
- Roy Waller (portrayed by Nicholas Cage in *Matchstick Men*)

You get the idea. A veritable concatenation of the villainous and the predatory. Certainly, when I began my late-in-life adventure as a salesman and entrepreneur, my idealistic and somewhat bohemian family didn't quite know what to say. They probably thought I had become apostate to all that was fine and good. A Faustian sellout to filthy lucre. A crazed lemming falling into the rat hole of venality.

But in reality, what makes a good salesman is the opposite of the amoral knaves of popular myth: you simply don't win in the long term by fooling people. You win through sincere care and concern. It is actually the selfish way to be. That is a naive but very real truth. Another truth? Salespeople are brave people. Being a salesperson means constantly wrestling with notions that people think you're slimy and out to cheat them, and keeping your head held high with the knowledge that you're actually out to help them.

There are a lot of assumptions about salespeople, which is why I chose to dedicate a whole section of this book to The Sale. No matter what type of company you have, chances are, you need to sell something. In fact, every person in your company should think of himself or herself as a salesperson. Including the receptionist.

The Best Approach to Any Sale

"Everyone lives by selling something"
- Robert Louis Stevenson

People want to fall in love. A good salesman should let them.

To explain what I mean by this, let me step backwards for a moment. The root of quality selling must always be in having something valid, something true, something genuinely helpful to sell. If you don't have this, don't even begin to try to sell. The core foundation of sales is providing value. If you try to sell something that doesn't have value, something you don't believe in, or worse— sell by misleading customers - you are dead. You are a servant of the devil. You are an apostle of the unsavory. You are Bernie Madoff. You are a fraud and incipient thief, as well as a killer of your own soul.

Perhaps this is obvious, but in truth, good selling begins with a moral choice to purvey a real value. It is essential to know this in advance.

But assuming the real value of your selling proposition,

salesmanship is really nothing more than helping people be selfish, helping people do the right thing for themselves. The salesman's job is to guide people to "fall in love" with what can raise them up. To help clients discover what can improve their lives and their businesses. To do this, you simply tell the truth and tell it fiercely and sincerely. At that point, you are doing your potential client a favor by revealing the truth, in much the same way a social worker or a minister seeks to serve and enlighten. There is no reason a salesman should look upon his profession as less than ennobling. (If you can't see your product or service helping people in this way, find a different product or service.)

"If you feel love, you have a motive for existence, a reason for action."
- Bertrand Russell (The Impact of Science on Society)

People intuitively respond to real value that is sincerely explicated. Unlike the popular clichés about salesmen, long-term sales success comes from focusing on service and candor in all aspects of the sales process. Sales is not about fooling people, despite our culture of increasing hucksterism, voyeurism, chimera, sophistry, and ends-justifies-the-means manipulation. A liar and a villain is eventually known by his works. Gordon Gecko aside, you don't successfully sell with deception and legerdemain. In addition to selling a helpful product you believe in, salespeople need to focus on service. This is another way to add value. I care deeply about service, although it is not a concept most of us associate with sales. Service brings to mind careers like the ministry, medicine, social work, teaching, counseling, coaching, research, philanthropy, psychotherapy—the pure helping professions. This is a far cry from the "careers" many people associate with sales; maybe one notch above a thief, a murderer, or a politician. But that's why focusing on service is so important. I ensure my staff places a high value on service as well, because I want our brand to have a connotation of being a team of helpers.

The image of the salesperson needs to change. Personally, I started out with a negative image of salespeople. That's certainly where I was many years ago when one of my friends asked me to take on a freelance executive sales project. My immediate reaction? Ugh! But years later, here I am. A salesman. And it is, for me, quite the opposite of Ugh! In fact, it is often a daily epiphany of insight, freedom, and life-affirming wisdom, as well as an opportunity for service. I realized that sales is, in fact, exactly the same as every other profession. It is a vocation that produces satisfaction and happiness for its practitioners (and brings worldly success) exactly to the degree it returns value to the world.

"Forget words like 'hard sell' and 'soft sell.' That will only confuse you. Just be sure you're saying something that will inform and serve the consumer, and be sure you're saying it like it's never been said before."
- Bill Bernbach, Founder of Doyle Dan Bernbach

Authenticity

"We have to dare to be ourselves, however frightening or strange that self may be."

- May Sarton

T.V. is often so shallow, staged, and scripted that the rare glimpse of authenticity cuts through all of the crap like a knife. Back in the early eighties, I recall watching Johnny Carson one night when actress Shelley Winters was the guest. Carson was obviously fond of her, as he frequently had her on the show. Winters flounced her fat amplitude out and sank heavily into the guest chair. As I recall, Carson began with something like, "So, Shelley, how've you been lately?" Winters paused a moment, gave a great sigh and said, "Well John, the problem with me is that wherever I go, I go too."[xxxv]

It was funny but also sad. Winters was a notorious neurotic whose problems with drugs and men often played out publicly for the world to see. Nevertheless, there was a compelling sincerity to her despair that was poignant and illuminating. She was deeply authentic in a morose and melancholic way.

Although this reality was sad for Winters, the "wherever I go, I go too" philosophy should be a good thing for stable people. It gets to the heart of what I feel is crucial in good salesmen—authenticity. It seems to me that personal authenticity should always be a primary and ongoing quest of the salesman for at least two reasons. One, it makes for long-term personal health. Two, it results in successful sales.

People like what is real; they trust realness instinctively. And there are a million different equally valid ways to be real. It's a lifelong task to imbue a rooted, unconscious integrity, or a "real selfness," to all interactions.

I have always been and continue to be distrustful of people who talk about magical sales techniques. Sales folk who turn to silver bullet solutions from various sales gurus will ultimately be disappointed. Because, like any other vocation, happiness and effectiveness for the salesman are only rendered dynamic and sound when placed on a bedrock of self-knowledge and integrated personal values—that is, an earned and lived integrity.

President George Bush, Sr. was visiting a nursing home in 1992 and he met an Alzheimer's patient. He asked the patient, "Do you know who I am?" The patient's answer was, "No, but if you go down the hall there's a nurse who can tell you." If only authenticity were that simple.

Another authentic person I especially admire is retired tennis player Andre Agassi. I watched him on 60 Minutes years ago and was deeply touched by CBS's excellent interview. In addition to being a fine piece of broadcast journalism, it limned Agassi's spiritual journey with a superb dramatic arc. The interview was hyped (along with Agassi's autobiography *Open*) on the revelation that he admitted using crystal meth for a year during his tennis career and lied about it to the powers that be. However, this rather minor revelation of a young man's sin, to me, was not what made the piece extraordinary. What made the interview powerful was that without real guidance or education (Agassi never graduated high school), he willed himself to become a deeply and profoundly authentic person—a person he didn't even know he was when he began his journey. His pilgrimage from liar, fake, and lost soul to authentic human wholeness struck me as particularly heroic in that it was largely internal, solitary, and autodidactic. A profoundly lonely but determined odyssey. While direct and confessional, Agassi was clear-eyed and without self-pity. Admirable. Even astonishing—and more astonishing for the fact that he chose his path from a place of unanchored anomie, ungrounded in faith or family.

One of my jobs when I was younger was teaching tennis, and I've continued to follow tennis over the years. Even before this remarkable autobiography and interview, I admired the grace, artistry, and passion of Andre Agassi. I admired his calm, his court savvy, his fierce spirit. Barbra Streisand called Agassi "the Zen Master." While I agree with Barbra Streisand about very little, I do agree with her about this.

So you may ask, "How can you know Andre Agassi is not just a big ol' self-absorbed phony out hyping his book?" Because I am a salesman. I can smell authenticity.

The simple key to successful salesmanship is authenticity. That soulful core is the pure essence of good salesmanship. A good salesman is authentic. He knows who he is. He tells the unalloyed truth from a centered space and people respond. I hope I am neither a naïf nor disingenuous when I state with absolute sincerity that authenticity is the key to selling. But you have to be authentic before you can sell authentically. Though not a salesman, Andre Agassi is a remarkable case study and example of achieved authenticity. So thank you Andre Agassi for becoming yourself.

Simplicity

"If you can't explain it to a six year old, you don't understand it yourself."

- Albert Einstein

I've noticed an interesting pattern in my sales efforts: If I try to sell everything, I sell nothing. Unfortunately, it's hard as hell for me to stop talking sometimes. In a sense, this is a case of "physician, heal thyself," as I am constantly pounding my clients to focus their sales message into a simple essence. When it comes to my own selling, it is a learned discipline to know when to stop. When it's your baby, every descriptive detail is a gem of rare price. But the fact is that loquaciousness is the enemy of illumination.

It's really true that most of the time less is more. I was reminded of that one Sunday in church, of all places. My minister told the following story in his sermon to illustrate a biblical point, but the story works fine as a lesson about simplicity.

Two ranchers from Texas are bragging to each other

about the size of their respective cattle-raising operations. One of them says, "Well, I've got 15,000 head of cattle out there on the range all wearing my 'Flying A' brand." "Flying A!" the other one sniffs. "My brand is the Bar T, Circle L, Cross Creek, Flying Z, Bent Fork, Double Back, North Canyon brand."

"Wow!" says the first rancher. "How many cattle are you running?"

"Well," the second rancher confesses grudgingly, "Not as many as you have. Most of mine don't survive the branding."

Courage

"The wise man in the storm prays to God, not for safety from danger, but deliverance from fear."

- Ralph Waldo Emerson

I'm a member of the International Wizard of Oz Club. (That's only one of my eccentric personal hobbies.) I've been a huge fan of the Oz books since my mother read many of them to me when I was a boy. Most people I know only read L. Frank Baum's first book, *The Wizard of Oz*, but there are actually 40 marvelous, magical, beautiful books in the series.

Getting to the point here, I have always loved the Cowardly Lion. He reminds me so much of myself. In the movie version of *The Wizard of Oz*, Dorothy confronts the Cowardly Lion and tells him he is nothing but a great big coward. The Lion's reply is: "You're right, I am a coward! I haven't any courage at all! I even scare myself. Look at the circles under my eyes! I haven't slept in weeks!"[xxxvi]

Boy, can I relate. For me to be an effective executive salesman for my company, I need to slay this "fear" dragon each day. To do this, I use a tip I learned many years ago from a wonderful acting teacher I had in New York named Michael Howard. Michael spoke one day about how to begin rehearsing a new scene. What he said was to go immediately to the most risky, scary, personal place in the scene, the place that made us feel most fearful and exposed. This might be a spot that involved physical intimacy, like kissing, violence, or nudity. Or jealousy, rage, or cowardice. By facing the most dangerous part of the scene immediately, the rest of the scene became more accessible, less fraught.

How do I apply this lesson when selling to my company's potential clients? By starting each day with the thing I want to do least. By immediately making that call where I have the greatest fear of rejection, where my own feelings of cosmic inadequacy might be most called out and exposed. In taking this sweaty-palmed action first thing in the morning, I *act* as if I have courage and confidence, and thereby gain it in reality. And the rest of the day is usually more pleasant and relaxing in comparison. I guess it's like a business version of your inner mother telling you to eat your vegetables first. For me, it works to go daily and immediately toward my most fearful task.

So go toward the danger. As the Cowardly Lion so

insightfully sings: "What makes a king out of a slave? Courage!"[xxxvii] Thank you, L. Frank Baum.

Charisma

"I call [charisma] the need to be authentic—or, as our dictionaries tell us, conforming to fact and therefore worthy of trust, reliance, or belief...[A person with charisma] is strong because he is what he seems to be."
- Daniel Boorstin

The Webster Dictionary defines charisma as compelling attractiveness or charm that can inspire devotion in others. Its derivation is the Greek word charis, meaning favor, grace, and rejoice.

Charisma is a quality that is frequently possessed publicly by some entrepreneurs, but not all. It can be hard to define but easy to notice. It's a leader's magical qualities. It's what makes the masses drawn to certain people— they have a universal energy that's infectious. People who truly know who they are and know what they believe release a compelling power that is almost religious in its nature. When thinking about charisma, many famous people come to mind, from John F. Kennedy to Ronald Reagan, to Bill Clinton to Barack Obama. Or actors like Clint Eastwood, Johnny Depp, and Clark Gable. Or tyrants like Adolph Hitler, Joseph Stalin, and Mao Zedong. These, and many other folks across numerous fields, seem to have a recondite knowledge attached to a public presence.

Certainly qualities like eloquence, pulchritude, and style are a help in enhancing charisma, but that's not how charisma originates. The essence of charisma is built on passion and commitment to a vision. My feeling is that charisma is innate in every human being and is a quality that can be cultivated.

The best example of unlikely charisma I can think of is Abraham Lincoln, who was possessed of a stoic stone face and odd body shape. Now thought to have suffered from Marfan Syndrome, Lincoln's enemies called him "simian" because of his unusually long, skinny limbs that gave an ape-like resemblance. He dressed only in black, dull, ill-fitting clothes, had an unkempt beard, and to judge from his photographs, seemed to never comb his hair. This off-beat man became the greatest U.S. president.

Entrepreneurs have a unique opportunity to grow into charisma because they operate in a vocational milieu of freedom. They take huge risks, and most fail. (Certainly

I, as an entrepreneur, wake up every day feeling a whiff of danger and fear in the ether.) But entrepreneurs also have the opportunity of connecting their unique inner truth and vision to truly new creations. In this sense, entrepreneurs can be closer to the sacred, in this secular age, than many ministers or priests. Like the religious man or the artist, their path is one of passion and verity.

The entrepreneurial salesman's chief task is to embody, in the sales process, the core truth of the product or service he sells. The great entrepreneurial salesman creates an aura of certainty and faith. When he leaves a room he leaves a sense of inchoate longing behind. This longing is not for a service or product, but for meaning itself. That is what a salesman like Steve Jobs possessed in spades.

Listening

> *"To learn through listening, practice it naively and actively. Naively means that you listen openly, ready to learn something, as opposed to listening defensively, ready to rebut."*

> **- Betsy Sander (former Sr. VP at Nordstrom)**

As I get older, I find my business style is becoming quieter. And I find this change is helping me as an entrepreneur and a salesman and a father. Take the latter role, for example. When I am in town, I read with and talk with my daughter almost every night before she goes to sleep. I used to try to guide her by talking to her about values or little lessons I felt I had to impart. I don't do that so much anymore. I've learned how to listen to her—*really* listen, until she asks me about something. Then we have real talk. This process has helped me as a businessman and a servant of my clients.

Listening is a critical business skill. (One thing that bothers me about social media is that it often seems to revolve around aggressive strategies of pushing out tweets, emails, links, etc., but not of real dialogue.) Yet who has not heard the 80/20 rule of sales—that you should be listening the larger percentage of time, and talking the smaller.

Listening is about discovery. My process of becoming a better listener and a better collegial entrepreneur has been one of giving up my preconceptions, my ego, my wish to control, and above all, my personal neediness. To react as more of a human *tabula rasa,* not a sales creature waiting to jump in and impress, and to let go of the effort of trying to read what people think of me. In a sense, this involves giving up and emptying myself before business or sales conversations. What other people think of me is none of my business.

This does not mean that effective listening is a passive process. It is active, concentrated, focused, and purposeful. As a leader, there is certainly a pressure to steer, control, and direct—to present a forceful image of being in charge. But I have not found that entrepreneurial leadership requires hegemonic assertion.

So how do we become more effective executive listeners? Well, I recently read a book by Bernard Ferrari, an ex-McKinsey director, called *Power Listening: Mastering*

The Most Critical Business Skill Of Them All. Ferrari feels that all of us are flawed listeners to one extent or another, either by having a hidden agenda of some sort or pretending to care when we don't. [xxxviii] He details the various listening offenses, and I must admit to having at least touched on most of these as leader and salesman of my company. I am actively trying to do better.

> *"There is no such thing as an empty space or an empty time. There is always something to hear. In fact, try as we may to make a silence, we cannot."*

> **- John Cage**

One thing that helped me make a lot of progress on my listening skills was a bad case of laryngitis. I could barely talk for a week and had to largely shut up. This gave me a lot of time to think about silence. My forced quietude, while frustrating, had a positive effect on me personally, and strangely, a salutary outcome on my limited sales interactions. I found myself very focused on being succinct and making my words count. Also, I found myself sharply concentrated on listening. It's quite centering. When I did speak, I was to the point and responsive to the particularity of my clients and associates. I simply didn't have the voice for bullshit.

I admit to occasional prolixity. It's hard for me not to throw in the whole kitchen sink when I'm talking about my wonderful company. I love my company. I'm passionate about it. Yet my health coerced stillness reminded me that silence is a necessary and efficacious value in sales, as in life.

Quite aside from my laryngitis, I've always found a judicious use of planned silence a help with everything. There are four things I personally try to do each week to create moments of stillness. Simple, but helpful to me.

- First, I go to church. That one hour of quiet thought and physical non-activity, sans cell phones, children, chatter, etc., is clarifying and revivifying (quite aside from deeper issues of truth and faith).

- Second, I try to take a half day every week to go to the movies by myself, where I can be alone in the anonymous dark. I try to pick intellectually undemanding movies (think American Pie, just about anything with Jennifer Aniston, Police Academy VI, etc.) Sometimes I go right to sleep, but frequently new thoughts come when I let go with no agenda.

- Third, I remind myself to stay aware of how much I really care about my clients and employees, and how they impact my world. It's not always easy to do, but it is the Polar Star of determining if I'm present, if I'm real, and if I'm true. It's a good place to keep coming back to in any meaningful business conversation.

- I formally meditate 20 minutes every morning.

As much fun as it can be to talk, listening is often much more valuable. When I take the time to listen to others, interpersonal relationships deepen and I feel myself grow as a person.

Don't Overdo It

"There is always optimum value beyond which anything is toxic, no matter what: oxygen, sleep, psychotherapy, philosophy."
- Gregory Bateson

Mae West famously said, "Too much of a good thing can be wonderful." Charming and witty as I've always found Mae, she's wrong.

Last year, I found myself doing a whole day of sales calls back-to-back. This wasn't so unusual, as I've been the chief rainmaker for my firm the whole time I've been in business. I'm pretty sure-handed with how I choose to represent my company. I know who I am and the business qualities I want to emphasize and convey. I'm articulate and passionate, as are most successful entrepreneurs. Yet there are times when my very strengths can undermine me. This was one of those days.

I found myself becoming a warped version of myself. Gradually and without quite realizing it, I turned into a mechanical imitation of Tim Askew, a sort of gobbling automaton. As I tired through the day, it became easy to lean too hard on what I really do well. The compelling positives of my approach and pitch (speaking bluntly and honestly) turned negative and harsh. In other words, I was a jerk, an asshole, a used-car salesman, a gold-plated phony.

We can cause damage to our business by over-valuing and over-relying on our strengths. When we lean too hard on our most wonderful qualities, there is danger in losing the balance that makes those qualities so wonderful. Too much passion and confidence can come off as arrogance. Too much restraint and patience can seem dull. And being too charming can verge on that slippery salesman perception so many people already have. We are all, of course, an amalgam of our strengths and weaknesses. Authenticity requires a constant need to be present with our whole self. And authenticity (telling the truth with our whole being) is the key to good entrepreneurial salesmanship.

So what should entrepreneurs do if they find themselves scurrying too often to strengths? Well, for me, I get out of my comfort zone. I have to stop and arbitrarily change my rhythms, become whole again, and realign. I have to get out of my chair, walk around, breathe, and click my heels together three times and say, "there's no place like home." Perhaps say a prayer for truth and wholeness.

Capitalizing on Your Weaknesses

"We succeed in enterprises which demand the positive qualities we possess, but we excel in those which can also make use of our defects."

- Alexis de Tocqueville

As with much of my business philosophy, my intuitions about sales are formed out of an autodidactic maelstrom of hit and miss, hunt and peck experiences---of getting it wrong a lot, till I finally began to get it right. In other words, I generally get good by being quite bad.

So essentially, my approach to life and sales is one of leading from weakness. By radically accepting my personal foibles, character flaws, wounds, emptiness, and inadequacy, I become paradoxically centered, whole, and compelling. My presence becomes a truthful and real thing by its very brokenness.

My doctor tells me bones grow back stronger after healing from a break, and I believe that persuasive sales presence emanates from a worked-through, self-accepting weakness. I'm not saying this approach is for everyone, but it is certainly the source of whatever success I have had as a salesman and as a useful human being.

I was reminded of this in a posting by my friend Reverend Stephen Bauman of Christ Church Methodist in NYC. He tells the story of Anna Mary Robertson, who worked as a hired girl on a farm. She met and married another hired hand named Tom Moses. They moved to a farm of their own and raised ten children. Ann loved to do needle work, but as she became older, her hands stiffened with arthritis. So she decided to try painting and found she could handle the paintbrush more easily. One day an art collector passed through her small town and saw her paintings in a drugstore.

She had been discovered at 77 years of age. She continued to paint until several months before her death at 101.

Reverend Bauman asks, "Why do we have the wonderful paintings by Grandma Moses?" His answer is that Grandma Moses was a crippled old woman whose hands were too stiff to embroider. In other words, out of her human handicap and frailty came her greatest accomplishment.

Sometimes what people see as weaknesses can actually

open the door for greater strengths. Out our flaws often comes our greatest power. Out of the muck of the pond emerges the beautiful lotus flower.

Working on Your Image: Manners, Vocabulary and Clothing

Now that we've gotten the state-of mind/character stuff out of the way, we should discuss the smaller things that shape the salesperson's image. These qualities are often falsely underestimated in the modern sales world. If you want to kick start your sales efforts, this chapter has a few simple solutions.

Manners

"Manners are the happy ways of doing things; each one a stroke of genius or of love, now repeated and hardened into usage."

- Ralph Waldo Emerson

Politeness, courtesy, niceness, manners. These are qualities I find increasingly missing in sales and most other aspects of business. Many people just don't see the need to bother with this stuff anymore in a rapid-paced social media world.

I was reminded of this a few years ago as I read Peggy Noonan's fine, zeitgeist-attuned article in the *Wall Street*

Journal, "We Pay Them To Be Rude To Us." Ms. Noonan states, "American culture is, one way or another, business culture and our business is service. Once we were a great industrial nation. Now we are a service economy." She says the social implications of this are making us confused and crazy. "We wear away the superego and get straight to the id, and what we see isn't pretty." She describes a revolution in manners. "We tore [manners] down as too fancy, or sexist, or ageist, or revealing of class biases. Just when we needed more than ever the formality and agreed-upon rules of manners to act as guardrails, we threw them aside. And now no one knows how to act anymore."[xxxix]

When I was a (mostly unemployed) young actor, I often supported myself as a catering waiter for high-society in New York. I worked for a company called Glorious Food, the most elegant caterer of the time. Glorious Food parties were run by a traditional and exacting maître d' named Serge. Serge was an old school martinet who was about doing everything with precise properness. Training to become a waiter for Glorious Food involved a long seminar where we were trained how to set a traditional table, fold napkins, correctly serve guests, etc. At the time, I thought this was a bunch of hooey.

But one day I found myself sitting next to the daunting Serge and got to talking to him about why we did all this minutia so precisely. He quite cogently explained to me that, as silly or unnecessary as it might seem to an American (think slight disdain with a French accent), there were very good and practically efficacious reasons for why the dessert spoon is placed over the desert fork, or why the white and red wine and water glasses were in a specific configuration; it made things easier for the server and the guest. It was not arbitrary or phony. It was well thought out and imminently practical.

There is a reason for manners and courtesy too, and it is not just to be nice. The purpose of manners is to give us a practical structure to deal with each other. It is not bullshit. It is the glue of civilization and the utilitarian road map for dealing in everyday business. Manners and polite address are not superficial. They are essential. The importance of plain good manners is rarely explained with any depth these days, including the workplace. Too bad. It is an important tool in the modern salesman's repertoire, and many don't have it.

Vocabulary

"I'd call him a sadistic, hippophilicnecrophile, but that would be beating a dead horse"

- Woody Allen

Words are wonderful. They are much more useful in business than they get credit for, particularly in executive sales. But words are not much emphasized or particularly valued in current articles and discussions I see about sales. These sales articles are crammed full of an overwhelming amount of information about psychology, motivation, technology, social media, ROI, SEO, etc., yet seemingly never mention that simple cornerstone of human communication—words. Vocabulary. It's as if words are unimportant or irrelevant to a modern salesman. Words are for poets and philosophers, academics and lawyers, journalists and judges. Words are old-fashioned. Words are of the past, supplanted by a world of Twitter abbreviations.

This is utterly wrong. And it is particularly untrue of high-end, quality business development. Word usage and proficiency is important in branding a tonality of equal business stature when selling to real strategic corporate decision makers. Top CEOs are especially well-educated, thoughtful people trained in the best schools in the world. Or, if they don't have that specific educational pedigree, they are fierce autodidacts. Either way, they are usually people of probing intellect and subtle ability to express and communicate nuance.

Corporate decision makers like to do business with their peers. They want to deal with people of equal business stature. A comfort level with precise and sophisticated word usage is one way of immediately establishing that tonality. However, this does not mean to pepper your sales conversations with artificially grandiose phrases, fustian excess, or arbitrary verbal whimsy. Precise vocabulary can be used simply. But words bring shadings of specificity and descriptive depth, even a sensual enlivening, to the most prosaic of sales conversations.

Sartorial Splendor

"Know first who you are; and then adorn yourself
accordingly."

- Epictetus

There is a famous German novella I read in college called *Kleider Machen Leute* by Gottfried Keller. (It is usually translated as *Clothes Make the Man*.) It's about a poor tailor who takes a coach journey, and through an odd set of circumstances, he is dressed in a fur-trimmed cloak much above his station in life and his real ability to afford. He is mistaken for a rich man. The results of this false identity and various people's reactions guide the tale.

This novella is highly applicable to entrepreneurs. I believe many entrepreneurs don't pay enough attention to their attire.

Clothes are important from a personal branding point of view. Potential clients and customers make quick assumptions about you before you say a word. Your clothes can make an eloquent statement about who you are and what you represent before you open your mouth.

119

Most of us spend large amounts on branding, marketing, and advertising to create the apt image for our firms. Yet it constantly amazes me how little thought owners give to how they present themselves. It is relatively inexpensive personal branding we're talking about here. And it most certainly does not mean an entrepreneur needs to be a fashion plate. Any styling from the funereal to the flamboyant can be appropriate, but it should be consistent with your chosen messaging and branding. Making strong, identifying statements through your attire can create a defined presence before you say a word. It can telegraph a context and corporate definition.

I've had clients who accomplish this bespoke branding very well in t-shirts. Some of my creative clients will choose bold colors. If you sell beer, you might want to look like a guy who is comfortable in a bar. I am sure Anna Wintour spends extensive time each day ensuring her personal clothes visually affirm her authoritative fashion leadership as editor of Vogue Magazine. Let me hark back here again to Steve Jobs. He wore black turtlenecks. This said a great deal about his personal values and the user-friendly elegance of his products. It spoke simplicity. He was who he was. He was sincere and spartan.

Personally, I try to look like a banker. For example, my firm, Corporate Rain International, is mostly known for creating high-quality meetings with real financial corporate decision-makers. My clients often entrust me with their most proprietary information and secrets, use my firm to initiate discrete, high-end business with c-suite people and corporate decision-makers. To look like I belong in that business, I need to look the peer of my clients. I want to create the visual assurance of stability. So, even though my personal history and proclivities are quite bohemian-hippie, I want to create assurance of stability and discretion. I do this partially by investing in high quality, well-tailored, expensive suits and by insisting that my associates always dress "high" when meeting with clients.

Tangentially, there was an interesting article in the *New York Times* entitled "Mind Games: Sometimes a White Coat Isn't Just a White Coat." The article cites a recent study concerning "enclothed cognition": the effects of clothing on the cognitive process. Dr. Adam Galinsky conducted a study that showed subjects who wear a white coat that they believe belongs to a doctor experience a sharp increase in their attention. Alternately, subjects who wear the same white coat but believe it belongs to a painter won't show any improvement in attention. Dr.

Galinsky states, "Clothes invade the body and brain, putting the wearer into a different psychological state."[xl] In other words, your clothes define you for other people, but they also define you to yourself and can affect your inner efficacy.

You don't need to hire a personal stylist or have a total makeover to accomplish inner and outer personal branding. You just need to think about it a little. It's common sense. If it serves your image to wear t-shirts, wear t-shirts. If it serves you to be elegant, be elegant. If it serves you to dress in drag, by all means, dress in drag.

Communication Tools – "New" vs. "Old"

"The ability to simplify means to eliminate the unnecessary so that the necessary may speak."

- Hans Hoffman

A big part of business is communication—not just the words, but the mediums. Entrepreneurs and salespeople today have more options than ever, yet many make poor choices in the tools and mediums they choose to use. For example, I loathe PowerPoint presentations. There's just about nothing in business I more dread. While I know many people feel the same, PowerPoint is acknowledged to be the most popular tool for creating slideshow presentations, and an essential sales tool for many of my entrepreneurial colleagues. There are well over 500 million PowerPoint users in the world, including over 30 million per day, and over a million going on right now.[xli] My guess is the majority of these presenters are boring their listeners to death.

I don't use PowerPoint (or any of its alternative cousins). Here's why: I want people to listen to me, wonderful me.

Admittedly, my company lends itself to a simpler presentation than, say, a complex, rococo technology sale. I don't necessarily need SmartArt flow charts to tell my story. Of course, I don't mean to be absurdly reductionist in my intuitive salesman's dislike of PowerPoint. Obviously there are necessary moments for the graphic and visual. But even when necessary, it should be kept simple, as should almost everything in sales---because, even when selling a complex product or service, buyers hire who they know and like. Anything that clouds or vitiates the urgency of that personal selling relationship is counterproductive.

The simple truth is that the more efficaciously naked you can be emotionally, the more compelling you become as a salesman. PowerPoint puts a layer between the salesman and the client that I prefer not to have. Selling without a slide deck makes it a more personal, courageous, and compelling act.

In a *Wired* article from 2003 titled "PowerPoint is Evil: Power corrupts. PowerPoint corrupts absolutely," Yale professor Edward Tufte, who is noted for his authoritative writings on information design in the field of data visualization, comments about PowerPoint: "Imagine a widely used and expensive prescription drug that promised to make us beautiful but didn't. Instead, the drug had frequent, serious side effects: It induced stupidity, turned everyone into bores, wasted time and degraded the quality and credibility of communication."[xlii]

That rather neatly sums up my sales instincts on the use of PowerPoint.

> *"Sir, more than kisses, letters mingle souls."*
>
> -   **John Donne**

Now, let us consider what I regard to be the opposite of PowerPoint—that antediluvian museum piece, the personal business letter. The top communication tool of another era, this quaint antiquarian form of business correspondence is a disappearing art form. It is in sad disrepute, condemned to ridicule and contumely by the go-go cutting edge of business. The idea of sending a personal letter is increasingly pooh-poohed (if considered at all) as an inefficient instrument of nostalgia and the past.

Let me be contrarian on this. It is my feeling that entrepreneurs are abandoning an important communication tool by dismissing the efficacy of the personal letter. Of course, entrepreneurs are not the only ones. The US Post Office is bankrupt because of a huge drop in letters of any kind (along with the innate lumbering inefficiencies of any government bureaucracy).

Certainly, most small businessmen are uncommonly busy. Emailing, tweeting, and linking in are faster modes of communication. Yet I also believe there is a certain emotional laziness to going too quickly to reaching out just through these insta-presto mediums. It is a personal thing writing a good business letter. It is a warm medium and can connect people on a more emotional level. Even a simple one-line thank you note does this. There's just something about thick, creamy stationary that says, "I care." but there are several reasons business folk are quick to abandon the letter:

1. Let's face it. Most businessmen don't write very well. Arthur Levitt, past Chairman of the Securities and Exchange Commission and Bloomberg columnist, has been on a jihad to bring good English back to business. He says much of business writing is cold, shallow, and lacking in nuance and color. It is boring to read.

2. A good letter requires energy to write with

compelling sincerity. A compelling letter means being open, vulnerable, and personal to some extent—even in a sales letter. While most entrepreneurs are passionate, harnessing emotions into meaningful, intimate conversations is not necessarily a common strong suit.

3. Writing isn't taught or remediated in business school. In fact, many high schools and undergraduate programs have de-emphasized English and writing to make room for emerging technology-related subjects. As more and more communication goes digital and becomes shorter and less formal, it's easy to see how it's resulting in the erosion of basic writing and vocabulary skills. (LOL, OMG, WTF, BRB.) U understand?

So why should the entrepreneur write more personal letters, especially in the sales process?

Well, I'll tell you why. Since people don't send letters anymore, when they get one, they notice it and actually read it. Unlike PowerPoint, which is so common that the mere mention makes people's eyes glaze over. A handwritten letter shows personal attention and a service orientation in the midst of an increasingly impersonal society. Even if your schedule is packed, it only takes a few moments to jot a sentence or two and sign your name, and it comes across as infinitely more thoughtful than an email.

"No" is Your Friend

"I wish I was less of a thinking man and more of a fool not afraid of rejection."

- Billy Joel

As a final point for the entrepreneurial salesperson, here's a simple, short thought: "No" is good. Obviously, "yes" is better, but "no" is a good second-best. The worst, a long and drawn out "maybe."

I frequently tell my friends that rejection is my middle name. For myself and any salesman, rejection will surely be the result of many, if not most, of your interactions. That is certainly the case for high-end sales initiation. When we're doing great, we will often still be getting 85 percent rejection.

A few years ago I was struck by a blog written by Anthony Tjan and published by the Harvard Business Review. Tjan is managing partner and founder of the venture capital firm Cue Ball. He is not officially in sales, but his thoughts are applicable to sales. He states, "A yes is obviously the answer you always hope to get, but the ability to get to no, especially if it is a quick one, is critical to maximizing efficiency and effectiveness. The sooner you get a no, the faster you'll be able to look for that next yes."[xliii] Utterly true.

Beware of ditherers and vacillators. They will eat you up. They are the real enemies of efficient sales. There are ways to cut to the chase without brusqueness, discourtesy, or antagonizing a real prospect. For example, one simple thing I try to do right away with new potential clients is ascertain if my firm's costs are manageable. Corporate Rain is a high-end service. With greatest courtesy, I always want to make sure a potential client can afford my firm before getting in too deeply. This respects his time as well as mine. But when your proposition is rejected, for whatever reason, it is important to keep focused on your core values. When I am rejected, I strive to become even more courteous than when a sale seemed possible. I try to keep my mind focused on service, even when there is no business to be had. This brands a seamless tone of helpfulness, good humor and collegiality that carries over to the next sales event, hopefully a more successful event.

Getting to "no" is a real sales value in itself. Tjan quotes a friend of his as saying, "…a fast 'no' is better than a long maybe."[xliv] Indeed. With this in mind, God bless the "no." Rejection can be a good and necessary part of sales. It is not a negative, it is a helpful efficiency. Handling rejection positively is a part of any healthy ongoing sales effort.

According to legend, the Greek philosopher Diogenes (412-323 B.C.) was seen begging from a statue. When asked the reason for this pointless action, he replied, "I am exercising the art of being rejected."[xlv] As should all good entrepreneurs and salesmen.

Part 4: The Future

Humility

> *"Humility is just as much the opposite of self-abasement as it is of self-exaltation."*
>
> **- Dag Hammarskjold**

In her book, *Stephen Sondheim: A Life*, Meryle Secrest quotes composer Steven Sondheim on his friend and colleague Leonard Bernstein's consistent failure to produce any significant music after his great masterpiece *West Side Story*. Sondheim says Bernstein developed "a bad case of importantitis."[xlvi] That is, anything he touched, by self- definition, had to have the weight and portent of the great.

Importantitis can sure be a killer of creativity and corporate health for the entrepreneur as well as for the artist. I was reminded about this by the dizzying fall from grace of Mark Hurd at Hewlett Packard, a man of achievement and power brought low by ethics violations and the apparent attitude that he was above the rules. (Or who can forget Leona Helmsley's famous statement that the rules—such as paying taxes—apply only to "the little people. "[xlvii])

Jonah Lehrer wrote an article on this in the *Wall Street Journal* called "The Power Trip," in which he notes what psychologists call the "paradox of power."[xlviii] That is, the very traits that help leaders rise to power disappear once they ascend. "Instead of continuing to be polite, honest, and outgoing, they often become impulsive, reckless and rude," says Lehrer. People with power become subject to hubristic overreach and Icarus-like arrogance. Lehrer quotes extensively from University of California, Berkeley, psychologist Dr. Dacher Keltner's scientific findings from studies of power and success. Dr. Keltner states, "When you give people power, they basically start acting like fools. They flirt inappropriately, tease in a hostile fashion, and become totally impulsive." Dr. Keltner goes on to compare the feeling of power to brain damage, stating that people with great power tend to behave like neurological patients with a damaged orbito-frontal lobe, a brain area essential for empathy and decision-making.[xlix]

An entrepreneur is usually a boss. He is a person of power, if only in his own very small pond. As such, I believe it is crucial to avoid importantitis. At Corporate Rain International, I try to guard against this in several ways. First, I never stop cold calling. At this point, I could have other people take over this task for me completely, but I want to experience what my associates and employees experience each day, which includes a great deal of rejection. Second, I hire people who I think are smarter or more experienced than me in certain areas and would be able to do their job at my company better than I could do it myself. After I hire them, I listen to their input, and typically defer to their expertise.

In an article by Patrick Caddell, a Democratic pollster, and Scott Miller, chairman of Core Strategy Group, they observe an increasing inability of executives to admit mistakes, including both Presidents George W. Bush and Barack Obama, and how un-useful a quality this is in an executive. They say, "As we've seen again and again over the past few years, admitting a mistake is almost constitutionally impossible for today's corporate chiefs and even harder for politicians."[1]

Humility is a business skill, but also a skill of great leaders. I was reminded by this recently when I watched *The King's Speech* for the second time. I was immensely touched by this movie and by the true story of King George VI, who accidentally became King of England upon the abdication of his older brother Edward VIII in

1936 on the eve of WWII. George VI was deemed imminently unsuitable to become a British monarch because of his debilitating and humiliating stutter. It was unimaginable that this man could inspire and lead his people with such a handicap. The film chronicles George's attempt to overcome this severe and very public embarrassment.

For me, George VI's story is a tale that informs and inspires me in my own attempts to lead a company from my own flawed foundation. Corporate leaders are all stutterers in one form or another. It is an audacious act to create a company despite the inadequacies that, in their variegated ways, are the fundamental heritage of all people. This is why I have always felt the foundational virtue of entrepreneurship is courage.

Colin Firth, who portrays George with an admirable combination of determined fortitude and raw emotional nakedness, describes watching archival footage depicting George VI's stutter. "You see the neck and mouth go. I found it heartbreaking, literally tear-jerking. Something really hit me watching that. I saw the vulnerability and immense courage, all wrapped up in one moment."[li]

George VI's story is a healthy reminder to my own Baby

Boomer generation. We have lost the valuation of practical modesty in business. George VI's predicament reminded me of today's best entrepreneurs: the combination of practical modesty with a frontiersman's ability to step fearlessly into the unknown. This is the quality of effective corporate leadership that I most admire. We Baby Boomers have devalued practical modesty. Many of us have come to think too highly of ourselves. We seem to have lost the innate humility that comes from an acknowledgment of our fallen, flawed nature, what we unapologetically used to call sin, the state of being less than God. Ideal corporate leadership is mindful of the practical reality of human limitation and imperfection.

The King's Speech gives a piquant reminder of the limitations in each of us as corporate leaders, as well as the earned dignity imbued from both the acceptance of that imperfect human state and its vanquishment where possible. Healthy entrepreneurial leadership exists in a balanced place between narcissistic overconfidence and an immobilizing despair at our inevitable insufficiencies.

Look at Me-ism and Smartphone Slavery

"Technology doesn't just do things for us. It does things to us, changing not just what we do but who we are. The selfie makes us accustomed to putting ourselves and those around us 'on pause' in order to document our lives. It is an extension of how we have learned to put our conversations 'on pause' when we send or receive a text, an image, an email, a call. When you get accustomed to a life of stops and starts, you get less accustomed to reflecting on where you are and what you are thinking."[lii]

- Dr. Sherry Turkle

I assume most everyone saw Barack Obama yukking it up at Nelson Mandela's funeral in 2013—he was taking "selfies" with other heads of state during the memorial service. While I assume President Obama admired Nelson Mandela as much as the next person, the tone he set made me uneasy and got me thinking about social media and its effect on the culture of the entrepreneur.

Self-obsession seems to be growing with the expansion of all social media, especially for those who become successful and well known. The selfie is just one of the latest manifestations of a culture that often confuses personal exhibitionism with business accomplishment. I call it "Kardashianitis"—visibility as a counterfeit version of value and vision. It seems to me this is a dangerous and distracting trend for entrepreneurs.

Psychologists Jean Twenge and Keith Campbell have reported the steady growth of self-importance in our personal lives over the last decade. They and others have described a burgeoning "narcissism epidemic" abetted by social media.[liii]

It's increasingly easy to confuse entrepreneurial exhibitionism with entrepreneurial success. That's why heightened ego is the enemy of practical business efficacy. It's distracting and disorienting. In this omnipresent culture of "look at me-ism," the useful tool of social media can be perverted into a quest for self-glorification. Look at how many "likes" I got, check out my retweets, look how many people have "friended" me this week, etc. Or look at the case of former New York Representative Anthony Weiner, hoist on the petard of his own scandalous messages and selfies. (These conversations are actually on display at the Museum of Sex in New York.) Weiner is a poster boy for this new apogee of self-ardor, seductively facilitated by use of social media. Weiner's downfall was not brought about by a sin of lust or passion, but rather a jejune exhibitionist search for public approbation.

According to Douglas Rushkoff, author of *Present Shock: When Everything Happens Now*, we're becoming addicted to a "dopamine squirt"—the ego boost we get from our Twitter, Facebook, emails, and texts. This leads to a compulsive immersion in the skittering superficiality of keeping current and cool on social media. Rushkoff says this is stress inducing, and, more importantly, creativity killing.[liv] I certainly agree that we are becoming committed to a sort of always-on, live-streamed reality show which is taking us into creatively shallow, spiritually thin cultural waters. In other words, technology is turning us into dull-eyed i-zombies who are not mentally present. Rushkoff feels we are losing the gift of reverie and connection to our fellow human beings, as well as to brain processes that summon non-rational revelations and Aha moments.

This point was brought home to me when I was in Dallas on business last year and found myself a bit lost and late to my next appointment. I looked for some friendly, authoritative face to approach for aid. But as I looked around, I found every person I saw shuffling vaguely along fully immersed in their personal private technology Idahos, inured to any person or thing around them. I didn't want to rudely interrupt, but I was annoyed because I needed some directions, dammit! This made me think about how much present richness and human feeling we sacrifice for an ersatz virtual reality. (I increasingly feel the same way walking down Broadway in New York when half the folks bump into you while texting, rather than taking in the infinitely unique international culture and urban magnificence constantly on display in my never boring city.) We are losing our real-life experience, our existential present, in order to miss nothing our machines bring us. Jaron Lanier, who popularized the term "virtual reality" in his book *You Are Not a Gadget*, says information is an alienating experience. People can only make sense of information and truly understand it if they experience it in the real world through human interaction.[lv]

There are several clear dangers in this infatuation with social media:

- First of all, it can be a distraction from your core commitment to your business passion and dream. It's easy to overvalue virtual vanity metrics, but they are often a time wasting diversion, and they vitiate and belie the deeper sense of integral self that is needed to execute our entrepreneurial vision. (We sacrifice our "eureka" moments for the present experience of superficial sledding on an omnipresent sea of technological connectedness.)

- Second, social media is often a bloody waste of time. Why are you looking at pictures of cats when you could be busy thinking about something that actually matters?

- Third, people just don't like self-aggrandizing assholes, the energy suckers of our vocation. You see the Likes your self-indulgent selfies and blogs get, but you don't see the eye rolls or hear the tongue-clicks from your "friends" who are sick of you.

So, I'll make you a deal: If you will not tweet about the excellent ham sandwich you had for lunch, I will forego posting a picture of my adorable labradoodle. This will help both of us stay focused on these things in real life, rather than on documenting them.

In the play "No Exit," French philosopher and dramatist Jean-Paul Sartre said, "You are your life, and nothing else." He didn't know it at the time, but "nothing else" includes your popularity on social media.

Pleasing Yourself

"Free at last! Free at last! Thank God Almighty, we are free at last"

- Martin Luther King, Jr.

Ricky Nelson wrote a hit song called "Garden Party" in 1972. The chorus and conclusion of the song goes like this: "You see, you can't please everyone, so you got to please yourself."

While I am a flawed businessman, I am a wildly successful entrepreneur. How does that work? Well, it is because I have achieved exactly what I intended through my adventure in entrepreneurship. Whether I have created a long-term viable capitalist entity can be judged by others over time, but I genuinely don't much care whether I've created a profitable institution for the ages. I'm in business because it makes me happy and free. It's a gas. It's a joy. It's an ecstasy of self-discovery. It is healing and whole-making and never boring.

My personal goals have never been financial. What I knew when I started my company in 1996 were my personal values and the tone of service I wanted my company to emanate. I knew I wanted to create a community I could comfortably live in and a safe place to recover from my addictions and past failures. I wanted a horizontal company inhabited by peers and fellow travelers, both in my associates and in my clients. I knew that I would be pleased if I could create this type of business, so that's what I focused on.

If truth be told, I'm not especially interested in business, per se. I've had no desire to be a master of the universe. What I desire is to be happy, centered, and whole, while running a healthy enterprise with integrity and freedom, and offering a real needed service to the world. Those are my reasons to be an entrepreneur. If I went out of business tomorrow, it would in no way adumbrate my personal sense of success and achievement as an entrepreneur. I've been doing what makes me happy for years. How could that ever be failure?

As an entrepreneur, don't stray from what makes you happy. That's why you're doing what you do in the first place.

Don't Get Lost Along the Way

"If you don't know where you are going, you might wind up some place else."

- Yogi Berra

It's good to know where you're going before you start trying to get there.

My minister tells great stories. He told my congregation one recently about Albert Einstein, who was notoriously absent-minded. I'll preface this story by saying it's *supposedly* true. (Ministers aren't known to lie.) Einstein was taking a ride on the Metro North train out of New York, and the conductor came by to collect the tickets. Einstein pats his pockets and can't seem to find his ticket. The conductor recognizes Einstein and tells him not to worry about it, and goes through the rest of the train collecting tickets. On his way back he sees Einstein on his knees on the floor frantically looking for his ticket. The conductor once again tells him not to worry—the fine for not having a ticket will be waved. Einstein looks up from the floor and says, "But I can't remember where

I'm going."

There are many things I do poorly as an entrepreneur. I am a poor administrator. I am impatient in meetings. I am not good with the quotidian details of spreadsheets and day-to-day financial analysis. I am a poor technologist. My personal organization is frequently inchoate. And this is but a short list.

Nevertheless, I've led my firm for nearly 20 years. The chief reason I've managed to get by is likely that I am very clear about where I want to go, who I want to be, who I want to have as clients, who I want as employees and associates, and what I want my brand to represent.

Harvard Business School I ain't. For example, when I started out, I typed my bills on an old Underwood typewriter. Even then in 1996, that pretty much classified me as a dinosaur. I knew nothing. But I had a clear view of where I wanted to be in five years, ten years, and fifteen years. I had a clear unalloyed personal goal. I knew where I wanted my personal journey to take me, and I didn't let myself get lost along the way. As naive a point as it is, it's really necessary to know where you want to go if you are to get there—personally, as well as professionally.

Again, duh, as my daughter would say.

Acknowledgements

First, I want to thank my friends, colleagues, and associates at Corporate Rain International for their encouragement and faith, with especial gratitude to executives Tom Cox, Sylvina Parker, Angela Maness, and Alex Albert. Amelia Forczak, my editor, was superb and graceful in ameliorating my utter ignorance about the technicalities of editing and publishing. Also, thanks to my technological guru, Rob Longley. Much appreciation to Eric Schurenberg, President and Editor-In-Chief of Inc. Magazine, and to my editors there, Rob Cantor and Jon Fine, for allowing me to develop my thoughts in a weekly column for Inc. Online. Many thanks to my mentors and friends too numerous to mention, but especially Tom Martin, Michael Drapkin, Bob Koncelik, Bo Burlingham, Patric Hale, Lewis Schiff, Carol Goman, Howard Moskowitz and the entire Inc. Business Owners Council of New York. Most of all, my extreme gratitude to Tracy Goss for her support and life-changing wisdom. Last, but hardly least, my profound gratitude to my long-time friend, Chip Spear, whose encouragement was seminal to this project.

Citations

[i]William Butler Yeats,"The Second Coming" *Michael Robartes and the Dancer: Manuscript Materials (The Cornell Yeats)*, eds. Thomas Parkinson and Anne Brannen, (New York: Cornell University Press, 1994).

[ii]Carl Schramm, "The Entrepreneurial Frontier," *George W. Bush Presidential Center,* December 16, 2012, http://www.bushcenter.org/blog/2013/02/01/entrepreneurial-frontier.

[iii]William Shakespeare, *Henry V*, ed. Gary Taylor, (Oxford: Oxford University Press, 2008), Act 1, Prologue.

[iv]Walter Isaacson, *Steve Jobs*, (New York: Simon and Schuster Digital Sales Inc., 2011).

[v]Maureen Dowd, "Limits of Magical Thinking," *New York Times*, October 25, 2011, http://www.nytimes.com/2011/10/26/opinion/limits-of-magical-thinking.html?_r=0.

[vi]Plato, *Phaedrus,* trans. Christopher Rowe, (London: Penguin Classics, 2005).

[vii]David Foster Wallace, "This is Water," commencement speech, Kenyon College, Gambier, OH, May 21, 2005.

[viii]Carl Schramm, "Teaching Entrepreneurship Gets an Incomplete," Wall Street Journal, May 6, 2014, http://online.wsj.com/articles/SB10001424052702304279904579515953479728072.

[ix]Steve Jobs, keynote introducing the iPad, San Francisco,

CA, January 27, 2010.

[x]Peter Cappelli, "Why Focusing Too Narrowly in College Could Backfire," *Wall Street Journal*, November 15, 2013, http://online.wsj.com/articles/SB10001424127887324139404579016662718868576.

[xi]Ibid

[xii]Michael S. Malone, "How to Avoid a Bonfire of the Humanities," *Wall Street Journal*, October 24, 2012, http://online.wsj.com/articles/SB10000872396390444799045780482302865033390.

[xiii]Kelly Greene, "New Peril for Parents: Their Kids' Student Loans," *Wall Street Journal*, October 26, 2012, http://online.wsj.com/news/articles/SB1000087239639044402420457804462264851610?mg=reno64-wsj&url=http%3A%2F%2Fonline.wsj.com%2Farticle%2FSB10000872396390444024204578044622648516106.html.

[xiv]Dr. Edward Hallowell, *Crazy Busy* (New York: Ballantine Books, 2007).

[xv]Patricia M. Greenfield, "Technology and Informal Education: What Is Taught, What Is Learned," *Science* 323, no. 5910 (2009): 69-71.

[xvi]Linda Stone, "The HBR List: Breakthrough Ideas for 2007," HBR, February 2007, http://hbr.harvardbusiness.org/2007/02/the-hbr-list/ar/1.

[xvii]Dr. Russell Poldrack, "How Multitasking Affects Human Learning," *National Public Radio*, March 3, 2007, http://www.wbur.org/npr/7700581/how-multitasking-affects-human-learning.

[xviii]Mihaly Csikszentmihalyi, *Good Business: Leadership, Flow, and the Making of Meaning*, (London: Penguin Books, 2004).

[xix]Sigal Barsade and Olivia (Mandy) O'Neill, "Employees Who Feel Love Perform Better," *HBR* blog, January 13, 2014, http://blogs.hbr.org/2014/01/employees-who-feel-love-perform-better/.

[xx]"Guiding Principles," PepsiCo corporation, accessed November 5, 2014, http://www.pepsico.com/Purpose/Our-Mission-and-Values.

[xxi]"Zappos Family Core Value #7: Build a Positive Team and Family Spirit," *Zappos*, accessed November 5, 2014, http://about.zappos.com/our-unique-culture/zappos-core-values/build-positive-team-and-family-spirit.

[xxii]Danny Meyer, *Setting the Table*, (New York, HarperCollins, 2009).

[xxiii]Danny Meyer, *Setting the Table*, (New York, HarperCollins, 2009), 189.

[xxiv]Edward Deci, Richard Ryan, and Richard Koestner, "A Meta-Analytic Review of Experiments Examining the Effects of Extrinsic Rewards on Intrinsic Motivation," *Psychological Bulletin* 125, no. 6:659 (1999).

[xxv]Mihaly Czikszentmihalyi, *Flow: The Psychology of Optimal Experience,* (New York: Harper Perennial Modern Classics, 1st ed., 2008).

[xxvi]Elizabeth Dunn and Michael Norton, "Don't Indulge. Be Happy," *New York Times*, July 7, 2012, http://www.nytimes.com/2012/07/08/opinion/sunday/dont-indulge-be-happy.html?pagewanted=all.

[xxvii]Edward Deci, *Why We Do What We Do: Understanding Self-Motivation*, (London: Penguin,

1996), 29.

xxviiiNassim Nicholas Taleb, *The Bed of Procrustes: Philosophical and Practical Aphorisms (Incerto)*, (New York: Random House, 2010).

xxixMonte Burke, "Head Games: Sports Shrink Bob Rotella's Advice for Winning," Forbes Magazine, November 10, 2007, *http://www.forbes.com/forbes/2007/1126/162a.html*.

xxxSue ShellenbargerXXX, "Better Ideas Through Failure," *Wall Street Journal*, September 27, 2011.

xxxiR.A. Dickey, *Wherever I Wind Up: My Quest for Truth, Authenticity and the Perfect Knuckleball*, (New York: Blue Rider Press, 2012).

xxxiiDoug Glanville, "I Am What I Throw," review of *Wherever I Wind Up: My Quest for Truth, Authenticity and the Perfect Knuckleball*, by R.A. Dickey *New York Times* blog, July 13, 2012, http://opinionator.blogs.nytimes.com/2012/07/13/i-am-what-i-throw/?_r=0.

xxxiiiIbid

xxxiv"All Happy Families," *The Sopranos* (HBO, 2004).
xxxv*The Tonight Show Starring Johnny Carson*. Guest Shelley Winters. NBC Productions.

xxxvi*The Wizard of Oz*. Turner Entertainment Co., 1939.

xxxviiIbid

xxxviiiBernard Ferrari, *Power Listening: Mastering The Most Critical Business Skill Of Them All*, (New York: Portfolio/Penguin, 2012).

xxxixPeggy Noonan, "We Pay Them To Be Rude To Us," *Wall Street Journal*, August 3, 2010, http://online.wsj.com/articles/SB100014240527487044 07804575425983109795768.

[xl]Sandra Blakeslee, "Mind Games: Sometimes a White Coat Isn't Just a White Coat," *New York Times*, April 2, 2012, http://www.nytimes.com/2012/04/03/science/clothes-and-self-perception.html.

[xli]"The problem with PowerPoint," *BBC News*, August 19, 2009, http://news.bbc.co.uk/2/hi/8207849.stm.

[xlii]Edward Tufte, "PowerPoint is Evil: Power Corrupts. PowerPoint Corrupts Absolutely,"*Wired*11.09, September 2003, http://archive.wired.com/wired/archive/11.09/ppt2.html.

[xliii]Anthony Tjan, "How to Get to No," *HBR* Blog, April 21, 2010, https://hbr.org/2010/04/how-to-get-to-no/.

[xliv]Ibid

[xlv]Clifton Fadiman and Andre Bernard, *Bartlett's Book of Anecdotes*, (New York: Little, Brown and Company, 2000), 168.

[xlvi]Meryle Secrest, *Stephen Sondheim: A Life*, (Illinois: Delta, 1999).

[xlvii]"Leona Helmsley," *Biography.com*, accessed November 06, 2014, http://www.biography.com/people/leona-helmsley-9334418.

[xlviii]Jonah Lehrer, "The Power Trip," *Wall Street Journal*, August 14, 2010, http://online.wsj.com/articles/SB10001424052748704407804575425561952689390.

[xlix]Ibid

[l]Patrick Caddell and Scott Miller, "ObamaCare and New Coke:

Presidents, Like CEOs, Can Pay a Steep Price for not Admitting Error," *Wall Street Journal*, April 24, 2010, http://online.wsj.com/articles/SB10001424052748703876404575200550394710626.

liDavid Mermelstein, "With Vulnerability and Fortitude," Interview with Colin Firth, *Wall Street Journal*, January 19, 2011, http://online.wsj.com/articles/SB10001424052748703333504576080622211651348.

liiDr. Sherry Turkle, *Alone Together: Why we expect more from technology and less of each other*, (New York: Basic Books, 2011).

liiiJean M. Twenge and W. Keith Campbell, *The Narcissism Epidemic: Living in the Age of Entitlement*, (New York: Free Press, 2009).

livDouglas Rushkoff, *Present Shock: When Everything Happens Now*, (New York: Current; Reprint edition, 2014).

lvJaron Lanier, *You Are Not A Gadget,* (New York:Vintage; Reprint edition, 2011).

Made in the USA
Lexington, KY
25 June 2015